WHEN CRISIS HITS SUBURBIA

A MODERN-DAY PREPPING GUIDE TO EFFECTIVELY
BUG IN AND PROTECT YOUR FAMILY HOME IN A
SOCIETAL COLLAPSE

TED RILEY

CONTENTS

Introduction   7
Author Profile   11
What will be Covered in This Book   15

1. WHEN INSIDE IS BETTER THAN   19
   OUTSIDE
   Knowing When and Why It Is Time to   19
   Bug In
   So, What Do I Take With Me on a Bugout?   21
   Building a Survival Headquarters   24
   Key Chapter Concepts: 28

2. EMERGENCY PREPAREDNESS BASICS   29
   Critical Information and Organization   29
   Your ERP   30
   Key Chapter Concepts: 43

3. ESSENTIAL #1 WATER   45
   Everything You Need to Know About   45
   Emergency Water Storage
   Key Chapter Concepts: 54

4. ESSENTIAL #2 FOOD   55
   Prepare a Pantry to Support Your Families   55
   Health, No Matter the Situation
   The Importance of Survival Nutrition   64
   Key Chapter Concepts: 65

5. ESSENTIAL #3 MEDICINE   67
   Make Sure Your First Aid Kit is Bulletproof   67
   List of Important Medical Books: 74
   Key Chapter Concepts: 76

6. ESSENTIAL #4 SECURITY   77
   Preparing to Protect Your Home and   77
   Community in SHTF
   The Importance of Establishing a Defensive   87
   Perimeter
   A Note on Firearms   91
   Key Chapter Concepts: 93

7. ESSENTIAL #5 ENERGY   95
   Are You Ready to Survive Off-Grid?   95
   Short Term Power Outage Preparedness   101
   Long Term Power Outage Preparedness   104
   Key Chapter Concepts: 110

8. ESSENTIAL #6 HYGIENE   113
   Are You Ready to Stay Clean and Deal With   113
   Your Family's Waste?
   The 6 Key Areas to Sanitation   114
   Pest Control   127
   Key Chapter Concepts: 131

9. IS EVERYONE READY?   133
   Teaching Your Kids Emergency   133
   Preparedness
   The Home Culture   136
   The Biggest Mistake   144
   Key Chapter Concepts: 146

10. THE BACKUP PLAN   147
    When Bugging in Needs to Become   147
    Bugging Out
    Bugout Bags and Contents   153
    Key Chapter Concepts: 164

    Conclusion   167
    References   171

A SPECIAL GIFT TO MY READERS

Included with your purchase of this book is your free
copy of the *Emergency Information Planner*

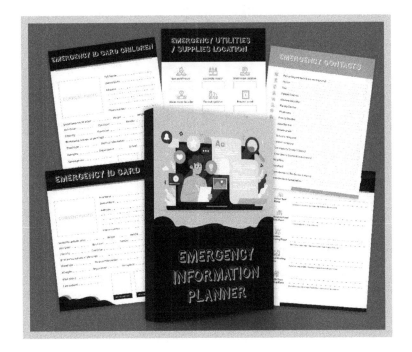

Follow the link below to receive your copy:
www.tedrileyauthor.com
Or by accessing the QR code:

Scan me

You can also join our Facebook community **Suburban Prepping with Ted**, or contact me directly via ted@tedrileyauthor.com.

INTRODUCTION

Extinction is the rule. Survival is the exception.

— CARL SAGAN

Your home is your ultimate survival investment. When chaos strikes, and we now know what chaos looks like, your home should be your primary survival shelter. Have you ever thought about your home this way?

These last few months have indeed been an awakening for many Americans. It might be the reason you are here looking over the pages of this book. I am humbled by your decision to use this book as a blueprint for hardening your home and protecting your family from an uncertain future.

Listen! You are more than capable of taking this on. You stand to gain so much by living a more prepared lifestyle. The actions you take are not just about SHTF. You will find that prepping for SHTF adds massive benefits to everyone living in your household. These benefits come from living a life that focuses on self-reliance and independence.

We are going to explore the very core of prepping and give you a clear direction on how you can get from where you are today to a place of preparedness and comfort in your own home. To get to that level, you will be required to bolster preps like food, water, medical, backup energy, and hygiene, and I am going to show you how to do that whether you have a large four-bedroom home or small apartment.

This Is the Knowledge You Can Expect to Gain by Following the Directions Given in This Book:

- You **will** be able to outfit and harden your home for maximum security
- You **will** build and stock a prepper's pantry to ensure your family eats
- You **will** prepare your children and teach them how to react
- You **will** be ready to go off-grid in a disaster
- You **will** have an effective evacuation plan
- You and your family **will** be able to survive the chaos if it comes to your suburb

How do I know all this? If you are going to stake your family's safety and security on it, it is a relevant question to ask.

AUTHOR PROFILE

My name is Ted Riley. I spent my formative years in the scouts, and I still remember getting that first badge for effectively using my pocketknife. I was hooked on the outdoors. Out there, I could swim in the water, build shelters, and start a fire! What more could an outdoorsy kid want?

I spent the weekends fishing with my father, and I learned a lot about woods and waters from him. Catching Summer bass while wading in the cool waters will forever be how I remember my dad.

When I was ten years old, we started moving around the nation and then the world. My dad had an incredibly unique skill set, and he had to travel all over to find and keep work. We didn't want for much as he was well-paid, but we were continually integrating into new environments. Some were safer than others!

We did a stint in Pakistan, and that was an experience I will never forget. The nomadic lifestyle taught me so many things about surviving in new environments. I quickly learned how to be noticed when I needed to be and how to disappear too! These are valuable skills you need to know if you are going to deal with chaos in the suburbs.

This was a radical way to grow up as a kid. In hindsight, it laid the base for my interest in survival and preparedness. The American safety net does not exist around the world. You might get pulled over by cops and forced to give them money. You might have the military come streaming down your street at a moment's notice.

These early life experiences are probably the reason I decided to settle down in Eastern Oklahoma. Here we are, homesteaders, pushing towards self-reliance and independence every day. Part of the motivation was to live a rewarding life where we take part in growing and caring for the food we eat and ensuring we are safe from calamity.

I do not doubt that my family will survive whatever comes our way in the future. We have created an environment that is built around preparedness. This has taken some work, but we are now in a place where every day is a blessing. When the storms of life come for us, we will be prepared.

Before finding my perfect home in Eastern Oklahoma, I spent years studying wilderness and urban survival. It was clear that this was my calling, and I enjoy the opportunity to share my knowledge. This led me to create a Facebook group where like-minded preppers can form a community.

Well, that's my story. Now we need to focus on yours. Are you ready to undertake something different? Are you prepared to face the future with confidence over fear? As I mentioned, I have no doubt you have the skill and the desire to make your preparedness goals a reality.

WHAT WILL BE COVERED IN THIS BOOK

THERE ARE A FEW ESSENTIALS THAT WE WILL BE COVERING IN THIS BOOK. THEY ARE THE FOLLOWING:

Water:

Most disasters do not affect the water system. However, in a societal collapse, we could see the tap run dry. If American taps stop producing water, people will struggle to stay clean, cook, and drink enough water to survive. We are going to talk about building a serious emergency water storage plan to ensure you have access to clean, safe water no matter the situation.

Food:

The more food you have, the better! Of course, it is not just about going out and buying all the food at the supermarket; managing emergency food storage is a process, and it can be one that changes your life and saves you money. This book will help you build a prepper pantry, create long term food storage, and even start growing your food outside!

Medicine:

The average residential medicine cabinet and first aid kits are not of a high standard. Most first aid kits are nothing more than some creams and bandages with a few packs of OTC (over the counter) medications. You can create a serious first aid cache with lifesaving medicines, tools, and skills to go along with it. We will also talk about managing things like prescription medicines in a societal collapse.

Security:

The principles of security are simple to understand. This book will outline how to harden your home and your community by using the concept of Detect, Deter, Defend. If you can affect these three principles, you can keep those around you safe.

Energy:

We are creatures who love energy. We use power every day with all sorts of things and do not even consider it. When the power goes out, it can be fun for a day, at best. After that, things start to get annoying, and then they get worse. There are many backup power solutions out there, and you can outfit your home in several ways.

Hygiene:

Another aspect of daily life we take for granted is personal hygiene. This is one of the reasons that disease and death are not as common as they once were. Personal hygiene preparedness can be handled pretty quickly if you stay ahead of it and access clean water.

Now you know what you are getting yourself into, let's get into it and get you set up!

1

WHEN INSIDE IS BETTER THAN OUTSIDE

KNOWING WHEN AND WHY IT IS TIME TO BUG IN

U nless you are tripping over stacks of money, you will not be able to reproduce the comfort, resources, and security of your home when bugging out. That is the most significant factor in all of this. Your home is more than you give it credit for. We are going to work together to take your home from the good survival investment it is to the ultimate survival paradise.

To best understand the potential of bugging in, we should probably talk for a moment about bugging out. When you bugout, you move from a no longer livable situation to a better, more livable location. One of the biggest hang-ups is deciding when it is time to leave. The best way to deal with this problem is to create triggers.

The use of triggers in survival and prepping is a great way to deal with all kinds of disasters. A simple example of a trigger is your fire alarm, which signals that you need to take action and evacuate your home to be safe. Another great trigger is the tornado warning. It tells you that you need to shelter-in-place away from windows, at the center of your home, or in a basement.

When it comes to the bugout, there are some very simple triggers that you can easily remember using the acronym REDOUT.

- **Resources**
- **Environment**
- **Destination**
- **Overwhelming Force**
- **Unpreparedness**
- **Threat Increases**

These triggers tell you it is time to bug out because your community is no longer safe for you and your family. Each trigger is unique but presents a serious threat.

Resources: There may not be enough resources available in your area, such as gasoline, food, medical help, and water.

Environment: Something like a nuclear meltdown or serious hurricane could create an environment that is dangerous to your health if you stay there.

Destination: While leaving your home for that bugout location might sound like a good move, you need to have an alternative destination. If you and your family bugout without a destination, you could do yourselves more harm than good.

Overwhelming Force: There could come a time when a riot or military or terrorist presence reaches your area and represents a force you cannot withstand. It is time for a strategic retreat.

Unpreparedness: You could face a threat you have not considered and therefore are not adequately prepared to withstand. This can happen to seasoned preppers. Sometimes something just pops up out of nowhere.

Threat Increases: While you might be managing your bug in just fine, the threat outside your home could increase to the point that it is no longer safe.

These are all serious situations that come with the risk of leaving your home and traveling to a new location amid chaos.

SO, WHAT DO I TAKE WITH ME ON A BUGOUT?

Building a bug-out bag to carry on your trip is a very personal undertaking. It is not as simple as just piling some of the most popular survival tools into a bag and ensuring it is filled to the brim. You have to first understand your bugout plan and location so you can know what you need in your bugout bag.

If your entire trip is 30 miles and you are taking that journey by car, there is no need to pack your bug-out bag with all sorts of water, food, and tools for building a wilderness shelter. If you are driving from point A to point B, you can pack pretty light.

Bugout shelters and sleep systems are a big deal. Building survival shelters is another exciting task that many people spend a lot of time on. Does your bugout require a shelter or a sleep system? Do you need a tent or a hammock?

We will go over some essential items that all bugout bags would benefit from. However, you should not assemble a bug-out bag until you have established a bugout location and route. These two plans will change everything, including how much and what type of equipment you bring as well as how you choose to carry all your preps.

Pump Water Filter:

While you might see straw-style filters and like the look of them, you can only use them at a water source. However, a pump filter allows you to fill containers or bladders so you can drink and travel. You will not always be able to find a body of water when you want a drink.

Self Defense:

If you are leaving your home because of chaos, it is vital to have a firearm or other means of defending yourself.

Seasonal Clothing:

Dressing for the weather is critical. You need to be warm when it is cold and cool when it is hot. Underestimating the elements will put a stop to a bugout, no matter how badly you need to get away.

Rain Gear:

When it rains, you have to stay dry. Moisture causes all kinds of problems, from skin damage to hypothermia.

Sunscreen:

While not a very cool bugout tool, sunscreen will protect you from discomfort. The sun can be brutal in a bug out situation.

Bug Spray:

Mosquitoes, mites, and other bugs can present a world of discomfort, just like the sun. Again, this is not a cool multi-tool, but it is a beneficial one.

Maps:

Paper maps are essential when you are on the road and bugging out. You could encounter any number of obstacles. Detours may happen several times, and you might not have the internet to automatically take you to your next detour.

Compass:

If you carry a map, you should also carry a compass and know how to use it.

Radios:

Communication is fundamental during a bugout. You might have a caravan of cars, or you might get separated into groups on foot. Radios will allow you to keep in contact despite the situation.

Flashlight:

You do not get to choose when the bugout takes place. If you did, it would be in spring when the weather is excellent. However, it could happen in the winter or in the dark, and you will need to have light.

The bugout should be your last resort, and you should focus your money, time, and effort on creating a serious survival headquarters in your home.

BUILDING A SURVIVAL HEADQUARTERS

While the situations above can incite fear and push you to the more radical fringes of prepping, remember that most disasters and emergencies will be dealt with from the safety of your home. That is where your support should be. If you dedicate yourself to creating a survival head-quarters capable of weathering a societal collapse, you could avoid the risky bugout altogether.

More good news: preparing your suburban survival head-quarters is not as lofty a goal as you might think. Most of the resources and skills you need can be acquired over time. You do not need to make a significant investment. If you can touch on each of these key survival priorities, week by week, you will start to see your level of prepared-ness improve, and your readiness take shape. Remember, this is a lifestyle of preparedness and not a one-time trip to the shops after which you store your purchases in the basement to be forgotten.

Water: You need 1-3 gallons of fresh water per person per day for drinking, cleaning, and washing.

Food: You need 2,000 (at minimum) calories per person per day.

Medicine: You need backups of prescription medicines and OTC medicine stockpiles along with skills and knowledge for treating illness and injury.

Security: You need to understand three security princi-ples: Detect, Deter, Defend.

Energy: You need to be able to charge essential electron-ics, cook, and regulate the temperature of your envi-ronment.

Hygiene: You need to be able to store essential hygiene items and may even learn how to make some!

Reading this book and being proactive will make all of the above possible. By developing these survival priorities, you will be more prepared to bug in during an emergency. These resources are crucial not only from a preparedness standpoint but also because these are the reasons people leave an area. Remember, the R in REDOUT is resources.

While not all disasters and emergencies will allow you to stay at home and bug in, many do. There are numerous benefits to facing off against a disaster in the comfort of your own home. If we are honest, these benefits far outweigh those you might have in a bugout situation.

Here are Just a Few of the Benefits That Go Along With Bugging in Rather Than Bugging Out:

- Unless any of your priorities are under threat, home is the safest place for your family in most disasters.
- A well-stocked home provides shelter, safety, and all the essentials you need to survive.
- Staying home provides a sense of normalcy, which is particularly valuable if you have children.
- It is easier to get quality sleep at home (which can't be underestimated in a societal collapse).
- It is easier to detect threats at home.

- Home offers the advantage of community relationships.
- When you are at home, your family knows where to find you.

Transforming your home into an effective survival headquarters, designed for a long-term bugin, is the goal. Of course, disaster could strike while you are at work or away from home. You could be forced to shelter-in-place at work due to some nuclear, biological, or chemical attack or emergency.

In this case, you will want to have a means of getting home if possible. This might require something like the construction of a get home bag (GHB). This bag stays in your car, and its sole purpose is to get you home safely in an emergency. When cars are not allowed on the road or threats have become severe along your route home, this bag should allow you to drive, ride, or walk home.

Most importantly, the decision to bug in, get home, or bug out should be based on good information. Multiple sources of information are best when you are deciding to make a life-changing decision like this one. Outside of news sources, there are ways to listen to police and fire scanners that can give you on the ground intelligence which will shape your reaction. If you can stay ahead of the herd, you will be set up for success.

School lockdowns can also be a big problem when you need to react quickly to a disaster. You will need to get the family together whether you plan to bug out or bug in. It is helpful to establish a meeting place if all hell breaks loose. This should be a safe and secure area where you can find your kids and know they will be safe regardless of the situation.

The tremendous benefits and practicality of bugging in are why you should focus on it as the nucleus of your emergency preparedness planning. The need to bug out may arise, and we will touch on that in chapter 10, but the focus on building your survival headquarters at home should be what moves the needle. Suburban prepping is definitely about resources, but community resources will be the most effective. You lose these resources when you isolate and bug out to the woods.

KEY CHAPTER CONCEPTS:

- Your home is your greatest survival shelter.
- A well-stocked and organized home is a prepared home.
- Treat your home as a survival headquarters.

2

EMERGENCY PREPAREDNESS BASICS

CRITICAL INFORMATION AND ORGANIZATION

When you see civil unrest on the news and feel that sensation of fear and desperation, it is easy to go right into buying. Buying food, water, guns, ammo, hygiene products can make you feel much better about where you stand in the world. If you take this path, you will find yourself panic buying or buying things you might not need in large quantities. You do not need everything right away, and if you begin to panic buy, this can become very costly.

Many preppers from my community have shared stories of their terrible decisions to purchase bulk items all at once. Usually, they find that they do not know how to use the equipment, do not like the food they have bought, or regret their purchases because their finances suffered due to their panic.

One case in particular sticks out more than most; it is the story of a young classically-trained chef who understood food better than most of the population. He used ingredients I had never heard of before and worked in some of the nation's best restaurants. His trip into preparedness had him reading all kinds of blogs and post-apocalyptic fiction. This chef's forays into the world of prepping had convinced him that he needed to store hard red wheat. This was the one ingredient he hadn't worked with, but he panicked and bought a lot of it!

Long story short, he realized he should have had a plan, and he should have stocked up on the foods he and his family ate every day. That is the power of fear. It can make you do things you would not normally consider. So how do you make sure that you do not get swept up in the waves of fear? Well, the greatest enemy of fear is planning, so you are going to create and refine your ERP (Emergency Response Plan).

YOUR ERP

Written plans are one of the most powerful preparedness tools you can create. They are often overshadowed by the allure of gadgets, guns, and body armor. When you are testing new gear, you feel a lot cooler than when you are sitting around with glasses on writing up your evacuation plan.

However, your ERP is one of the most important preps you will undertake. Not only does it offer up clear steps for when disaster strikes, but it also gives your family an invaluable tool if you are not around.

The fact that you are reading this book means that you are likely the head of preparedness in your household or you plan to be. The head of the household's biggest mistake is to run their home like a military operation and not share their knowledge, plans, skills, and training with the other members. If you were lost to the chaos, what would your family do? Would anyone be equipped to take up the reins and be effective? To successfully protect yourself and your family, everyone must be able to, to some degree, manage without you.

You have a lot of knowledge and information in your head that your spouse and kids may not. The Emergency Response Plan offers your family a means to survive by understanding the step-by-step plans they need to take in several disasters and emergencies. You could also include survival guides, first aid information, and other essential documents in your ERP.

Depending on how much you enjoy writing, the Emergency Response Plan may be a fun weekend or a nightmare; regardless, it must be done! You could use a simple freelance writer to put together your ERP if you do not feel confident writing your own. Of course, this presents many issues if you are tight on OPSEC (operational security). Even if you hate the idea of sitting down and writing, take the time. It will make a huge difference.

ERP Layout

The layout of your ERP is vital so that you can help your family navigate the document's innards. Your ERP may have 50 pages of information, and your family will only be accessing this ERP in the worst-case scenario. They may not have tons of time to leaf through your creation. This is why I like to take my time with it and show my family each section I either include, modify, or remove from our ERP. By doing it step by step, you give your family the best possible chance to understand both the layout and your thinking. Having an ERP night where you spend hours filling your family's heads with information that they will most likely forget is not the most effective way to introduce them to the plan. By doing it step-by-step, your family may have ideas and solutions to problems you have not considered. Adding in their ideas helps create a family unit and validates every family member you aim to protect.

Example: An emergency alert buzzes on your phone, and you find out that a nuclear power plant, of which there are 99 across the nation, has had an accident and resulted in a nuclear meltdown that may or may not affect your area. If you are at work, your family will want to know how to respond. An index or a tab, or both, will give you quick access to the Nuclear Emergency Plan.

Plans like these are not something we can expect our family just to have logged in the back of their mind. Let's look at the basic layout of a sample ERP. Remember, you can craft this any way you see fit. Just keep remembering that it should be easily accessible.

Location of Emergency and Disaster Essentials:

- Blackout kit
- First aid kits
- Fire extinguishers

List of Important Numbers for Emergencies:

These numbers should be neighbors, emergency services, family members, and anyone else who could be an ally or essential service in a disaster or emergency. You may already have these on your phone. However, if your phone is compromised, is it wise to have a backup, hard-copy available.

- Family and Friends
- Phone Contact Trees for Schools and Organizations
- Business Contacts
- Day Care
- Kid's Schools

- Kid's Friends and Families
- Doctors and Specialists
- Work Numbers
- Non-Emergency
- Utilities

Fire Drill:

Your fire drill is something that should be practiced regularly. This drill will dictate how your family deals with a fire in real-time. The fire drill should be tailored to the specific layout of your location. However, the following well-known sequence is a tried and proven drill that can be adapted as required.

- Stop
- Drop
- Roll

Shelter-in-Place:

There are many reasons your family might need to shelter-in-place. You should identify a location and pile everyone inside to ensure it is a good fit. Do not forget your pets!

Evacuation:

Sometimes you just have to go. Evacuation is quite different from a bug out, but we will get to that later. However, evacuation is important. Sometimes anarchy can be avoided by going to stay with some family for a few days.

Regional Preparedness Plans:

Every region has unique threats, and these threats need to be addressed in your ERP. Hurricanes, Wildfires, and Earthquakes are just some examples.

Bugout Plan:

The bugout plan is a serious undertaking. If you take the time and invest the money in executing a bugout plan, be sure you document everything.

Base Defense Plan:

Now, more than ever before, it is easy to understand the importance of securing your neighborhood. A base defense plan is used to create a perimeter and other important locations around your area.

Basic First Aid Resource:

There are a lot of first aid kits for sale. You can go to any drug store or chain store and find a few varieties. Some of the best kits at places like Target and Walmart include merely a few types of bandanas, cold compress, tweezers, ACE bandages, some creams, maybe a few bandages, and minimal OTC meds. If you are going to be medically prepared, you need to create a first aid cache.

Caching first aid supplies is a crucial part of preparedness. The problem is most Americans do not have a good understanding of basic first aid and treating people who are wounded, so they buy the kit, and most never open it or explore it! You need to add to your first aid cache some very important things, but you also need to know how to use them.

The modern first aid kit does not put anything in the kit that could potentially cause harm. Sometimes you need something like a tourniquet, which could potentially cause harm if left on too long. Sometimes you need something like a decompression needle to drain the blood from a punctured lung.

You should not invest in this type of equipment if you do not know how to use it. Therein lies the problem when it comes to first aid in the average person's home. We do not practice any kind of first aid or train it or learn it! What's even worse is the fact that your community offers CERT training at least once a year, and you can learn all of your first aid basics, but many people don't take this opportunity.

There are also higher-level first aid and trauma courses around the nation that are popping up more and more. These are an investment, but you will learn how to use things like chest seals, tourniquets, and decompression needles. These are lifesaving tools, but you need to know how to use them and understand that some can do more harm than good in the untrained hands.

You should also have access to a decent first aid manual. It does not have to be a MERCK, but it should be a comprehensive guide to dealing with injuries and trauma. CPR, Shock, breaks, sprains, and the like should all be addressed in the manual you choose. The reason for a small manual is so that you can stuff it down into your cache. When you build your first aid cache, it should be a one-stop-shop for everything you need.

Start with a medium to large-sized Rubbermaid container. This container should be able to fit the full scale of your most important, in-home, first aid items.

What Goes Into a First Aid Cache?

- Any previously purchased first aid kits
- OTC meds that your family uses and might need
- Thermometers
- Electrolyte Powders
- Rolled Gauze
- Nitrile Gloves
- Medical Tape
- Shears
- Peroxide
- Neosporin
- Rubbing Alcohol
- A variety of bandages with a focus on 5x9s

- Israeli Pressure Bandages
- QuikClot Gauze
- N95 Masks
- We also keep an essential oils kit

This is the making of a serious survival cache for your home. This is a container that you can grab and throw in a car if you need to bug out but can also be brought to a victim in need of treatment. If you are busy rifling through a closet or struggling to find what you need in your medicine cabinet, it could take away from precious time.

In many emergencies and disasters, the first responders are simply overwhelmed. We have seen this during the pandemic. This means you and yours might become the medical staff. Are you prepared for that?

- Prescriptions
- Blood Types
- Pre-existing Conditions
- Allergies
- Previous Severe Injuries
- Doctors Contact Information

These are all examples of vital documentation that you need to have on hand in an emergency. Each of your family members should have a card with this information on it. This will save medical staff precious time in the event of an injury sustained during a disaster. You will also be able to refer to this information yourself if you become the one treating the person you love most!

We will dig deeper into medical preparedness in our later chapter on the topic, but understanding and caching medical supplies and information is essential for good organization and efficiency.

Vital Documentation:

Whether you know it or not, there is a collection of documentation that proves you are who you are, and you own what you own. We rarely use this kind of documentation, but you will need all of your important information in the event of some serious collapse. You may have to prove who you are and what belongs to you at a moment's notice. You might have to prove that your children are truly yours!

Having this documentation or copies of it is a powerful first step in reacting to a disaster. If you have to leave your home in a hurry, this is the type of information that you need to have on hand. If your home is washed away by flooding water or torn down by civil unrest, the recovery will be much easier if you have all your important documentation.

Proof and Legality Documentation:

- Licenses

- Social Security Information
- Military Record
- Birth Certificates for ALL family members
- Immigration Records
- Adoptions Records
- Credit Card Info

Medical Information and Documentation:

- Immunizations
- Medical History
- Prescriptions
- Insurance Information

Insurance Documentation:

- Insurance Policy
- Local Agency Office
- Insurance Cards
- Home Inventory of Valuables

You could also gather together legal documents like your power of attorney information. A small document safe is the best location for these copies unless you have copies of your emergency response plan. Then you have it all in a one-stop location. I like the safe because you can store things like cash, silver, gold, ammunition, and even a firearm safely, and in the event of an emergency, you can grab it and go!

A simple thumb drive filled with digital copies of these documents is an excellent backup in case something were to happen, and you no longer had access to the hard copies or if you didn't want to turn over an original to someone you didn't trust. The thumb drive can be loaded with survival information, too! You can build a de facto survival thumb drive in an afternoon.

No matter where you decide to store your vital documents and backup copies, just know that this puts you one step ahead in how you react to the chaos in your community. The speed of your reaction will make all the difference if you are trying to stay ahead of crowds and calamity.

Checklists and Organization:

If you do not know what you have, you can never know what you need! The point of checklists is not about defining what you need but understanding the gaps in what you have. If you look at checklists to buy more things, then a checklist will be longer than it needs to be and wind up costing you significantly more than you need to spend.

Your checklists should also be uniquely yours. While using a basic checklist to start is fine, you should modify that list to add the items that are important to you. Keeping your preps organized is another key to your preparedness success. Just imagine that you are forced out of your home by a disaster or emergency. You are going to want to take as many of your preps as you can fit, right? Organized tubs, caches, and containers filled with preps make loading up the car more comfortable.

Conducting a quarterly inventory of your preps will keep your stockpile fresh. Do not forget to include the bugout bags and get home bags in this inventory. Everything should be checked, and any holes should be filled.

Sample Checklist:

- Bottled water
- Food supplies (as a starting point, FEMA recommends enough for 72 hours, but a minimum of a month would be a better idea)
- Way to purify contaminated water
- Camping stove
- Can opener
- Emergency heating (e.g., wood stove - something that does not rely on the grid)
- Emergency candles (also non-grid-reliant - e.g., candles, lanterns)
- Batteries & torches
- Basic tools
- Local maps
- Solar-powered charger
- Battery/solar-powered radio
- First aid supplies
- Hygiene supplies
- Your family's emergency bugout bags

- Reliable transportation (with spare fuel)

KEY CHAPTER CONCEPTS:

- Administrative tasks are the first element you should prep.
- Create a home ERP.
- Hard copies of important information should be recorded and kept in one place where everyone can access it.
- Information should be backed up using technology.
- Be sure to include several threats that are unique to your area.
- Run drills to ensure your family is prepared for possible threats.
- Invest in at least one comprehensive hard copy first aid resource.
- Create a detailed evacuation plan and checklist.

3

ESSENTIAL #1 WATER

EVERYTHING YOU NEED TO KNOW ABOUT EMERGENCY WATER STORAGE

Modern preparedness has many parts and pieces, and the scope is growing! This is good news because it makes prepping as rewarding as it is effective. However, just as the First Nations People who built their homes and villages near bodies of water, we understand that water is our number one essential when it comes to prepping.

This can seem crazy because we have a tap that gives us limitless water on demand. It is also very rare that we get a boil water notice and even rarer that the tap water flow is disturbed and our faucets run dry. Because of this, the American people get complacent. You get used to safe drinking water access! It is a marvel of modern society.

However, once that tap runs dry, you have about three days before your internal organs start shutting down due to dehydration. This is what we preppers worry about. Sure the water is everywhere, but when it goes away, the clock starts ticking, and if you do not have an answer, you are either going to flirt with death or have to line up to get rationed water.

To avoid that, you are going to create your emergency water storage solution. While that might sound pretty intense, I can assure you that you will have a bulletproof plan and be ready for water shortages or tap water outages in the future with some simple steps. To achieve this, we are going to focus on four core actions and items.

- Water Storage
- Rain Catchment
- Grey Water
- Water Filtration and Sourcing

Water Storage

One of the easiest steps you can take to prepare for a water crisis is to purchase extra water or water storage containers. If you have the room, you can store a significant amount of water in your home. Of course, you have to know how much water you need. This is simple. You just calculate 3 gallons of water per person per day.

If you know anything about water storage, you might be thinking, 'I thought you only needed 1 gallon of water per person per day?' If we are just talking about hydration, you are right. However, we also have to consider things like cooking, cleaning, and hygiene. In preparing for chaos and disaster, you will store lots of dry food, and that food will require water. If you start pulling from your one gallon of water per person to cook rice and beans, you will either have crunchy beans or thirsty family members.

There are also several places that you are already storing water or could store water in a hurry. One of the most popular storage locations for water is the bathtub. Filling bathtubs is an emergency imperative when preparing for things like hurricanes.

Your water heater and that fire hydrant down the street are both going to be great places that you can source water from your immediate area.

We are talking about 12 gallons of water per day or 360 gallons per month for a family of four.

It is unlikely that you will have the space to store all of that water in your home, but buying gallon jugs and water battles can provide convenient access to safe drinking water in an emergency. You might also consider totes or something like Water Bricks, which are large containers designed for holding water. These can be stacked, and as long as you keep them out of direct sunlight, you can store tap water in them.

Water storage is an important part of your emergency water plan, but realistically it is only one part.

Rain Catchment

The beautiful thing about water is that it falls out of the sky! There is no other resource that is so readily available. The problem is most people do not take advantage of this falling water. They simply watch it wash down their guttering, down the street and into the rainwater drains or through their yards and into the valleys, creeks, and streams that surround their home.

When you think about a number like 360 gallons, it might make you nervous. You can buy 55-gallon rain barrels for around $100 each. There are several varieties. You can also buy 55-gallon, food-safe barrels and make your rain barrels for less than that. Since these barrels hold 55 gallons of water, you can see how quickly those gallons add up after heavy rainfall. With four rain barrels hooked up to your downspouts, you will be able to hold 220 gallons of water just in those four barrels!

The water that drips into your rain barrels is not ready to drink. It will pick up contaminants rolling off your roof and sitting in that rain barrel. You should always filter and boil your water from your rain barrels. This is the best way to keep your family safe. Now, using this water for things like cleaning is much easier and does not require filtering.

Rain catchment is not limited to rain barrels, and you can create any kind of system you like. It is really up to your imagination. You can bury a 1000-gallon cistern in your yard and run a couple of downspouts to it. That would take care of all of your water needs.

You can also catch rainwater off other structures like outbuildings, sheds, chicken coops, and detached garages. When it comes to water, you want to use all of the available resources.

An effective rainwater system can handle a large portion of your emergency water needs.

Grey Water

We waste a lot of water in this nation. We let the hose run, and we take big hot baths. We wash dishes, and that water goes right down the drain and is gone back to the water supply.

However, on homesteads all across this nation, some people collect the water that goes down the drain in a bucket while washing hands or dishes. That water is called greywater and can be used to water gardens, water compost piles, and even complete outdoor cleaning jobs. The amount of water that you can save by using greywater is tremendous.

While catching greywater in buckets can be effective, it can also be a backbreaker! The more efficient homesteaders have created a greywater system that goes directly from the faucet to a cistern or straight into the garden. A simple valve can be used for this purpose. Take a look at your water needs and see if greywater can be something you take advantage of.

Water Filtration and Sanitization

Water collects sediments and pathogens quickly. Most concerning are bacteria and parasites. Giardia and cryptosporidium are two examples of things you want to filter out of your water to make it safe. If these bacteria collect and reproduce in your intestines, it can create serious gastrointestinal illnesses. You will suffer from painful cramps and diarrhea. If water shortage is an issue, then ailments like these will make hydration even harder to achieve.

Every day thousands of people die on our planet because they drink contaminated water. Clean water access is a serious issue, but it is one Americans are far removed from. Water filtration technology has come a long way in the last ten years, and you can now carry a highly effective water filter that filters down to .03 microns or small enough to block things like bacteria and parasites from making it through.

A micron is smaller than anything you can see with the human eye. It is smaller than a white blood cell, red blood cell, and even bacteria. When you filter with a quality water filter, you are using a diameter that is .03 of a micron. We are talking seriously microscopic!

Many filter designs work great and are effective in dealing with bacteria, sediment, and parasites. They might be straw designed, water bottles with contained filters, drip-style filters, or even hand pump style. You can even spend $1000 on a whole house filtration system. Just be sure you stock up on extra filters for your systems.

At the very least, you need a hand pump option. While products like the LifeStraw look great in brochures, you need the ability to refill things like water bottles, bladders, and maybe even pots for cooking. You simply cannot do that with a straw style filter.

The Katadyn Hiker Pro

This filter is what I carry in my bugout bag. It is a powerful hand pump filter that has filtered my water through many an adventure. It is easy to use and lightweight.

HydroBlu Pressurized Jerry Can

This little jerry can filter over 10,000 gallons of water and pump it out into drinking glasses or even a pressurized spray nozzle to wash up or clean. It carries 3 gallons of water and has made a home for itself in our emergency water preparedness plans.

Medium-sized water filtering solutions are essential. No matter which of these technologies you decide on, you need at least one. You could invest in a larger scale water filtering option.

You can also purchase water purification tablets to kill pathogens in your water. Bleach can be used as well; 6-8 drops of unscented bleach per gallon of water can act as a sanitizer for water.

Just remember that any water you catch or source from local streams, no matter how clean it looks, must be filtered, and it should be boiled for 10 minutes too. Remember, the most significant threats in water are too small for the eye to see. You cannot look down into a glass of water and see the pathogens swimming around.

Water Sourcing

Beyond catching and storing water, you also need to know where you can go to source water. I mean springs, wells, or bodies of water that can provide you with a source that will not expire, should be a part of your emergency water plan. From these bodies of water, you can either filter at the water source or you can collect water and process it back home.

Plotting out these water sources can be as simple as printing out an overhead view of your immediate area. Look for streams, creeks, ponds, and rivers in your area. These are all viable water sources. They can be marked on a paper map and visited to get a lay of the land.

The best source of water for drinking is going to come from running water that is deep enough that you can source from just below the surface without picking up sediment from the bottom of the waterbed. The surface of water bodies is contaminated, and most contaminants settle to the bottom. So, you want to pull water from the middle column of the water.

There are things like pollutants that can contaminate bodies of water, and these could be present if you need to move to a different body of water. Know what is upstream from your water source. You want to be careful not to pull water downstream from a business that dumps into the body of water.

Also, pay attention to runoff when you are looking at water bodies and water sources. If you can identify two to three sources for emergency water in your area, you are going to be in good shape if you ever face a water shortage or crisis.

When it comes to emergency water preparedness, you want to focus on options. You want as many options for water as you can muster. The more ways you can source and filter water, the less of a problem you will have staying hydrated in an emergency.

While it might seem like a lot, you can secure your emergency water needs in one weekend! The purchase of some bottles of water, a couple of rain barrels, some mapping of water resources, and the investment in a water filter that will filter down to .03 micron will give you all kinds of options.

Hydration is essential! Water on its own will not replace electrolytes, so you might also want to include some powdered electrolytes that can simply be stirred into the water and used to replace those things you lose when you sweat. It is all around us. It falls from the sky. Do not be caught without safe drinking water for you and your family.

KEY CHAPTER CONCEPTS:

- Store some water in the home but not the majority.
- You will need 80-90 gallons of water per person per month.
- Take advantage of rain catchment for the majority of your water storage needs.
- Consider the advantages of capturing and using greywater.
- You need a supply for drinking, cooking, cleaning, and washing.
- Have multiple methods of filtering and sanitizing water in your home.
- Identify at least one large body of water in your area as a potential long-term water source.

4

ESSENTIAL #2 FOOD

PREPARE A PANTRY TO SUPPORT YOUR
FAMILIES HEALTH, NO MATTER THE
SITUATION

The darkest parts of the 20th century were tied, in some way, to the scarcity of food or resources. The Soviet Famine starved millions of Russians and Ukrainians in the early 20th century. The Great Chinese Famine in the 50s was the deadliest in history and took the lives of some 22 million Chinese people.

Americans live a life of convenience with massive agricultural systems in place to keep supermarket stores full and a steady supply of grain flowing. In 2020 we witnessed what it feels like to go to a supermarket and see empty shelves. We saw shortages in meats, produce, and even dry ingredients.

If you set up a proper food storage plan that features a nutritious pantry, you will not worry about short term food shortages. They won't even phase you! To pull something like this off, you probably think you need thousands of dollars to spend on extra food. You probably think you need to be a master organizer. Neither is true. It is pretty simple.

The reality is that most American households have less than a day's worth of food to sustain the family in an off-grid emergency. In other words, most foods need to be cooked, and you need electricity or fuel to cook these foods. What does that look like in your home? If you factor in real nutrition, how do the ready to eat foods measure up?

Let's look at the four major areas where you can be effective with your emergency food preparedness.

A Prepper's Pantry

The prepper's pantry is designed to be a deep food storage solution for your family. It is important to understand that you are merely adding more of the same food to your cabinets and pantry that you already have on hand when you start building your deep pantry. In other words, if you usually have two cans of pasta sauce in your pantry, your goal should be to expand on that exponentially! This can be done by simply buying one extra can or packet each time you go to the supermarket.

If you buy one extra box of pasta and one extra can of meat sauce each week, you will have 12 easy emergency meals in 3 months. This will add about $3 to your weekly bill depending on where you shop. You can add extra cans of soup, rice, and oats to your weekly purchases too! In no time, you will begin to see the swelling of your pantry. When you have extra food on hand, you will immediately sleep better!

Remember, this expanded pantry should be made up of food items that your family already enjoys. Do not go out and buy food that your family doesn't like just because it has a long shelf life! Your pantry should be filled with weekly meals and snacks. Be sure to include a variety of foods so that you have a balanced diet that maximizes nutrition.

To supplement this pantry diet, you could also beef up your vitamin supply. This should include extra vitamins for adults and children. You might also consider storing protein powder as this can provide your family with essential amino acids if you find meat becomes a scarcity.

Building a robust emergency pantry will not be a financial strain. It will become a test of your focus and commitment. By spending $10 - $20 extra per week, you will begin to see the results in a matter of months, and this is only one aspect of how you address your emergency food storage needs. When SHTF in Suburbia, you and yours will be eating, not having to scramble for food at the store or be forced to eat unhealthy alternatives.

Organization and Rotation

Adding all of this extra food to your home will require you to focus more on the organization of your pantry and the rotation of food. You should always be eating the oldest foods first, and to do this, you need to understand the concept of FIFO (first in, first out). Popularized by the food industry and food safety standards, FIFO is the process of moving out the oldest food first.

FIFO - First In First Out

The simple labeling of shelves can aid this type of organization and rotation. If you know where a specific item goes, it will be easy to understand how much you have. Then it will be easy to pull all of that product forward so you can add the new can, box, or bag behind the oldest food.

If you do not commit to your growing pantry organization and rotation, you will find yourself throwing lots of food out. Lack of organization could also bring pests into your home. Pests will wreak havoc on your food storage and your family's confidence in the food that is stored. If everything has to be inspected for chew marks from a rodent, it will be a big problem.

A simple weekly rotation of foods and occasional cleanout and inspection will keep your food safe, and in an SHTF situation, you will be cooking meals just like you were before the chaos took hold.

Emergency Dried Foods

Some people build up food storage by purchasing freeze-dried meals that come packed safely in containers. These can be stacked and stored anywhere you see fit. They also have a tremendous shelf life. Most of these companies will promise a shelf life of around 20 - 25 years. In the last five years, some of the best emergency food companies have even expanded the variety of foods offered to include things like non-dairy and vegan options. The market is growing, and people are buying these foods every day.

Here is a list of some of the best companies that are selling these foods right now.

- Legacy Foods
- Augason Farms
- Emergency Essentials
- My Patriot Supply
- Wise Food Storage
- Shelf Stable Foods for Long Term Food Storage

DIY Long Term Food Storage

While these companies produce a great product, you too can make your 5-gallon buckets of long-term food storage. It is simple and, thanks to club buyers like Costco and BJ's, you can buy large quantities of discounted food.

Using Mylar bags, oxygen absorbers, and 5-gallon buckets, you can take advantage of discounted food prices and make your own long term food storage.

We store 5-gallon buckets of foods like beans, rice, oatmeal, sugar, and flour. These long-term food storage options are still one of the best investments I have made in my preparedness. It is the kind of nutritional insurance that is ready when disaster strikes.

So how do you do it? Let's look at the simple steps of bucketing up your long-term food storage.

Materials Needed:

- 20-50lbs of dried food (We will use a 50lb bag of rice as an example)
- 5 Gallon Buckets
- 5 Gallon Mylar Bags (These can be purchased online)
- 2000CC Oxygen Absorbers
- Hair Straightener or Iron

Method:

- Set out your 5-gallon buckets and open up your Mylar bags inside the buckets.
- Open your rice and use a clean coffee cup or large scoop with a handle and start filling a mylar bag that is settled into a 5-gallon bucket.

- Fill the Mylar bag about 4/5 of the way, leaving enough of the bag empty so it can be sealed.
- Before sealing, you must drop in an oxygen absorber. This will keep your food safe, dry and kill any bugs packed with the grain.
- Mylar bags can be heat sealed; you can use a hair straightener that is warmed up or an iron to seal these bags.
- Once your bags are sealed, you can place the lids on top, and you have a 5-gallon bucket of long-term food storage!

Stack these in the basement or garage, and you will have some serious food storage in the worst-case scenario. Do not forget to label and date these but be creative. A small label on the bottom might tell you what is in the bucket, and a larger label on the outside might read PRIMER, CEILING PAINT, or something else so that people will never suspect these buckets are filled with food.

Backyard Supermarket

The push to grow food has gripped the nation, and more people are gardening and community gardening than ever before! This inspiration has come from things like the COVID-19 outbreak and its effect on our food supply. Alternatively, the contamination of our food supply with pesticides, and the overall feeling of accomplishment that comes with growing your food, has been used as motivation.

You would be surprised at what you can pull off on a typical urban sprawl with some kind of simple fence to protect from things like deer. Before we had kids, my wife and I spent a brief time living in the suburbs of Virginia. I always loved Virginia. We were on 3/4 of an acre, and I cleared some of it for the man who rented us the property. We used that new space to spike our food production.

In the early days, we had a few raised beds in the backyard and a bunch of potted plants. As we got to know our soil and improved it, we began planting potatoes, squash, and heavy producers like tomatoes, peppers, kale, and cucumbers. We even raised green beans and English peas at varying times of the year.

We had a pretty impressive garden. We grew plenty of potted herbs too. In three years, we had added six laying hens in a small coop, two peach trees, an almond tree, a fig tree, a few different types of perennials, and even grew some shiitake mushrooms in the woods just behind us.

Are you the type of person who looks at the modern homesteaders and yearns for that kind of independence? You are capable of far more than you think!

Growing food takes time, most suburbs are allowing a small amount of laying hens, and no one is going to give you trouble over some fruit trees! Before learning about what you want to grow, you have to understand things like your soil and how to feed plants. You also have to know about the pests and wildlife that will assault your backyard gardens.

While traditional growing and raising animals works well, you could also invest in a hydroponics or aquaponics system that will produce food for you using a water-based growing system. Aquaponics systems will even provide you with fish that are raised right in your backyard!

You have a lot more options than the small garden bed with tomatoes and peppers.

Drying and Canning

If you get your backyard garden and growing systems up and running, you will quickly realize that you cannot eat it all! Even a small tomato garden will have you handing out tomatoes because you will get sick of those things in the high volume that they produce.

Investing in a dehydrator will allow you to dehydrate that backyard harvest. These dehydrated vegetables can be added to your stockpile or mixed with other dehydrated food items that can be combined to create quick meals.

Canning is another great way to take advantage of that backyard harvest. You have the ability to cook down foods, pack fresh, and do all sorts of cool things before canning your foods. Once these food items are safely canned, they can become a part of that growing pantry of yours.

If you get into canning, just be sure that you have a high-quality book or resource you can trust. Canning certain foods will require a pressure canner. Foods that are canned improperly can be dangerous to the health of your family. There is no point in putting up all this food if it is going to cause your family harm.

Preservation has a place in your emergency food plan. Never throw food away again!

THE IMPORTANCE OF SURVIVAL NUTRITION

So much preparation can get muddied by fantasy. While it might be exciting to consider trapping and hunting for food or subsisting off scavenged canned goods without labels and the like. If you want to be at your best, you are going to need to have balanced nutrition.

In an SHTF situation, you are going to be tested more than you ever have been. You are going to be physically and mentally tested, most likely, beyond your limits. You will not be sleeping because of fear and stress, and other routine items will not be happening either. If there is one area that you can positively affect, it is the overall nutrition of your food storage.

Over the last five years, we have seen some incredible studies to suggest that good nutrition and physical fitness can help with battling depression! In an SHTF situation, you better believe there will be some level of depression.

The lack of medications could also exacerbate poor health symptoms, and a good clean diet has been shown to improve things like diabetes. If you can create your emergency food supply from a prepper's pantry, long term food storage, and a garden of fresh fruits and vegetables, you will have a solid base.

While Mountain House is quick and easy, it is not the best form of nutrition. MREs store well, but they are not something you want to eat week over week for every meal. The needs of the human body do not change, even though the surrounding environment does. Keep that in mind while you plan your food storage program.

KEY CHAPTER CONCEPTS:

- Emergency food storage begins with a robust pantry filled with the foods you already eat regularly.
- Long-term food storage is designed to give you a safety net and, when appropriately packaged, can last up to 25 years.
- Your backyard or balcony can become a supermarket of its own if you create a viable gardening area.
- Canning and preserving will make your homegrown food supply go even further.
- Do not forget to rotate your food, first in, first out.

5

ESSENTIAL #3 MEDICINE

MAKE SURE YOUR FIRST AID KIT IS BULLETPROOF

We all have bodies, but few of us know how to take care of them. Isn't that crazy? Well, it is not when you think about it. We live in homes we do not know much about, and we drive computerized cars we couldn't fix in a million years!

First aid and medicine are specific skills that have hard limitations. You can learn to do a lot for someone who is injured, but there are things like surgery that you just cannot do unless you are trained. You will likely put the person at more of a risk by trying.

Of course, in an SHTF situation, we are going to be dealing with injury and illness with limited supplies and limited or no access to medical care. That is a serious consideration. When a child is suffering from an injury or illness in bed, and you do not have what you need to help them, everything gets very real.

My travels around the world showed me the austere situations that many people live in across the globe. The human body heals, and it is a marvel, but you should store the right kinds of medical equipment to help it along.

Building a Medical Cache at Home

Most retailers carry "Family" first aid kits. These kits are large and contain a lot of nothing. They are full of items that should be used to restock your first aid cache at home but are not a standalone solution in your home. Of course, having one of these is better than not having anything, but building a medical cache takes more time and thought than a small first aid kit you buy at the store.

Your medical cache will be crafted to meet your needs. You should consider your family members as well. This is the collection of first aid, medical equipment, and medications that you will need to care for your family when you become the doctor! That is a scary thing to consider, but it could quickly become a reality in an SHTF situation. The following list gives you an idea of the types of things you and your family would benefit from having in your first aid cache.

Bandages and Bleeding:

- Medical Tape
- Nitrile Gloves
- Rolled Gauze
- Gauze Pads
- Trauma Shears
- New Skin
- 5 X 9 Abdominal Gauze Pads
- Styptic Powder
- Tourniquets

Ongoing Wound Treatment:

- Splints
- ACE Bandages
- Rubbing Alcohol
- Peroxide
- Triple Antibiotic Ointment
- Aloe Vera
- Essential Oils
- Irrigation

OTC Meds:

- Acetaminophen
- Aspirin
- Anti-Inflammatory Meds
- Anti-Diarrhea

- Cough Suppressant

Prescriptions:

If you are on any type of medication, you need to sit your doctor down and talk to them about how you can get even more of your prescriptions filled. Maybe you can get three months of them in advance.

Of course, the bigger idea is to look at your health, diet, and fitness level and see how you can maximize these. You may just be able to get away from some of these medications with modifications to your diet and exercise.

The Bugout Medical Kit:

We have already established that bugging in or living out an emergency in your home is the best plan A that you can have. However, we wouldn't be preparing for much if we didn't have a plan B. Plan B for most preppers is going to be some kind of bugout. If your home becomes untenable, you will want an option that is your home away from home. You need a place where you can go to outrun the chaos and get back to living.

You will not be carrying your entire medical loadout with you on most bugouts. However, you still need solutions for injuries and illness during the bugout and at the BOL (bugout location).

Carrying medical equipment and first aid on foot is a lot of added weight, and you have to be smart about it. The best method for carrying serious medical preps on a bugout would be to either build or invest in an IFAK (individual first aid kit) for each family member. The IFAK will give you the ability to spread the weight out amongst the group. This is better than having one person weighed down with all the supplies, especially if your group gets broken up.

IFAKs can be purchased and should include bandages, tourniquets, pressure dressing, hemostatic agent to help blood clot, and other lifesaving implements like chest seals. In an IFAK, you should also have simple Band-Aids and ointments to deal with simple wounds, cuts, and scratches.

OTC meds are also great to add to your IFAK. The small packets are the best for this. Be sure to include the things that your family needs. Always have an answer for pain, fever, diarrhea, and congestion.

You could also create a secondary medical cache that could be buried at a location along the way. This means you could carry very minimal first aid along the way and just pick up your medical cache at a particular location when you get closer to the BOL.

Dental Care:

Dental care in SHTF situations is not as complicated as you might think. Now, dental surgery is just that, surgery. So, you should get this stuff handled before any foreseeable chaos hits. Schedule your surgery now if you need it.

Day to day dental care can be handled in several ways. It can be exciting to use survivalists and primitive tactics to care for your teeth and gums. You can just buy a tube of toothpaste every other week at the supermarket and then buy an extra toothbrush once a month. In no time, you will have the basics of dental care in large quantities. Throw some floss in there from time to time, and you will be well set up.

That said, we should also look at several ways that you can naturally affect your dental care in an SHTF situation.

Baking Soda:

This is a great toothpaste when mixed with water. It is simple, cost-effective, and has whitening agents.

Ash:

In Africa, it is very common for tribes to use the ash from their fire to brush their teeth. It might seem primitive, but many cosmetic companies have begun putting activated charcoal in some versions of their toothpaste.

Salt Water:

Simple salt water can do a lot to irrigate and cleanse your mouth. Of course, this assumes you are storing plenty of salt!

Essential Oils:

Essential oils can be added to things like baking soda to create an even better toothpaste.

SHTF dental is not a big issue unless you have a history of bad oral health. Take care of your teeth now! Get into the dentist and get things handled. If it comes down to SHTF dental surgery, just know it is going to hurt. If you know someone who has dental training, you should get to know them a little better!

EDC First Aid:

In an SHTF situation in the suburbs, you might consider carrying first aid wherever you go. I have been carrying a kit of my own for years—a simple kit to deal with things you might need to deal with while you are out.

Carrying things like activated charcoal, Swat Ts, Tourniquets, basic bandages, and some Band-Aids as well as some ointment, sunblock and bug spray, rolled gauze, and tape.

Instruction:

All around the nation, there are tons of classes teaching advanced first aid and trauma care. These courses cost money, but they are hardly the only resource if you do not have the money to go to these classes.

Your community offers a free CERT class at least once a year to help the community learn first aid. This could be a training opportunity for you, and it can be a way to solidify your skills each year and also meet like-minded people.

Books:

There is no substitute for hard copy information when it comes to medical and first aid. There are some books out there that anyone preparing for a medical SHTF situation should have in their library.

LIST OF IMPORTANT MEDICAL BOOKS:

The Survival Medicine Handbook

Dr. Bones and Nurse Amy have been THE voice in the prepping world for SHTF medical care. This was the first book written by Joe Alton M.D, aka Dr. Bones, and touches on everything you need to know about this topic. This is an all-in-one manual.

The Doomsday Book of Medicine

Dr. Ralph Laguardia has put together an incredible book that touches on all aspects of health, wellness, and medical care through the lens of surviving Doomsday. This book goes way beyond simple medical advice and techniques. It also introduces natural remedies and things like using common household ingredients such as baking soda to treat injuries and illnesses.

Alton's Antibiotics

There are some illnesses and injuries that just require antibiotics. You cannot get around it. The average person has no idea what to use and how much of it to use. This book takes care of all of that. It even teaches you how to acquire antibiotics.

Preppers First Aid Handbook

William W. Forgey is a veteran outdoorsman and a full-time practitioner of family medicine. This book is one of the most important. Learn how to deal with things as simple as bites and stings or as wild as building an off-grid medical kit. This book is a must-have for anyone interested in building a medical library for SHTF.

These are examples of great books that should be in your collection. Not to be confused with your first aid manual, these are designed to be for situations that call for more than basic first aid.

KEY CHAPTER CONCEPTS:

- Invest your time to create a high-quality first aid kit that is tailored to your needs.
- Make it part of a larger first aid cache full of items you and your family might need in a disaster.
- Outfit cars, backpacks, and vacation homes with quality kits.
- Consider SHTF dental in your medical plans.
- Invest in an SHTF first aid library that can be your reference if you become the family doctor.

6

ESSENTIAL #4 SECURITY

PREPARING TO PROTECT YOUR HOME AND COMMUNITY IN SHTF

Traveling around the world and throughout this nation, I have seen how people live and how safety and security play out differently in different areas. Some communities are guarded by gates, walls, and armed security. I have visited other places on the planet where villages are little more than grass and mud huts with minimal, if any, security.

Throughout history, we have been a people of fortifications and borders. Most nations realized that to remain secure and sovereign, an active military and secure border were essential. Kingdoms of the past went as far as building many walled defenses where attacking forces would have to hurdle several walls to breach the city.

We are living through a time of extraordinary peace in our nation. Sure there are criminals, there will always be criminals, but we are safer now than ever before. Of course, in SHTF, that can all go away, and things can get ugly in a hurry.

You do not need a three-walled defense around your castle, but there are some simple steps you can take to make your home significantly more secure. We are going to discuss the essential security principles in this chapter.

The Importance of Security in SHTF

It is hard for Americans to understand a situation that would be labeled as SHTF. What would the world be like without law enforcement, food, water, and medicine after about two weeks? Can you imagine the chaos in the streets? We have only had glimpses of what this might look like, and it is terrifying. Look back to events like the '92 riots in LA or the events following Hurricane Katrina's fallout.

These glimpses give Americans pause, but few take action to fortify their homes or establish anything beyond a few weeks of vigilance.

To put it simply, the majority of Americans are not prepared for widespread civil unrest. We are untrained and inexperienced. That is a testament to our society and the relative peace we have seen in recent decades.

I need you to understand that you and those around you will become the security detail in an SHTF situation. All the layers of protection, from the police to alarm systems, will dissolve, and no one will be coming to help you. That is the level of importance of this chapter.

The 3 D's of Home Defense

Thanks to our innovative military, there is a system in place that makes almost every aspect of emergency preparedness easier. When it comes to security and defense, there is one system that is easy for anyone to understand and to act on.

These are the 3 D's of Home Defense and Security:

- Detect
- Deter
- Defend

Using these three principles, you will be able to take actionable steps on any threat to your community or home. Once you have a plan, everything gets a lot less nerve-racking.

Detect

The detection of a threat is the first step in this system. This identifies a problem, a person, a group, or something else that just does not fit. There are two degrees of detection. The simple version is peeking out the blinds and seeing someone walking the streets late at night that you do not recognize. My mother was a champion at this method! She was always in those blinds. You could also be actively detecting threats by using things like cameras, trail cameras, or even drones to monitor your property.

You can look at detection from the standpoint of a home-owner. How best can you detect threats from your home? However, detection truly works best at the community level. A community threat detection system can be as simple as a communications network like the Nextdoor App and a few vigilante neighbors. As long as you can detect and report, you have a powerful system in your community.

Here are Some Great Tools for Detecting Threats in and Around Your Home:

- Optics (binoculars, monocular, night vision)
- Security Cameras on the Home
- Trail Camera
- Other Community Members
- Late Night and Early Morning Walks
- Perimeter Alarms

Detection is step one to understanding the nature of the threat you face. It could be an immediate threat, or it could be someone scoping your home or community out. Without detection, you could be unaware, and then it might be too late to react. There is a reason that we place defend at the end of this system. Detecting and deterring can be very careful.

If you decide to neglect these, it will also be awfully hard to be in the most advantageous position. Through detection and deterrents, you can identify a threat and give yourself ample time to consider the best way of dealing with that threat.

Deter

When you think about an SHTF scenario in suburbia, you go right to the AR15 and an ample supply of ammo. You invent a terrifying threat in your head, and then you consider the quickest way to mitigate that threat, whether that be a bunch of guys at your doorstep or a single intruder breaking in to steal food or to hurt your family.

It is quite common for preppers to get engrossed in firearms. Firearms can be a solution to a very severe problem, but the truth is, there are several ways that you can deal with threats to you and your property. The strategic prepper will spend most of their time on deterrents when it comes to home security.

Deterrents are practical and straightforward, and they can go a long way when it comes to avoiding severe security threats. With the overreliance on firearms, it is easy to forget that when you start firing rounds at a person, they could begin to fire rounds back!

Better than any tricked-out rifle is the ability to force the mind of a criminal to look away from your home without taking any action yourself. This comes from careful and strategic deterrents that have a psychological effect on the people casing your house.

This might all sound way too complicated. Maybe you are not a strategic person, but you like the idea of avoiding a firefight and setting your home up in such a way that the bad guys avoid it. To simplify all this talk of strategy, I am going to give you one sentence to consider.

Your home should be less desirable than the other houses on your block!

It comes down to desirability. Take a look at the homes around yours. Focus on them. Maybe take a walk and look at the yards, fences, and entrances to the houses. Then you need to start thinking like a criminal.

- Which house would be the easiest to break into?
- Which house could you break into without being seen by others?
- Which house provides the best way out without being seen?

These are all the types of things that criminals consider when they are casing a property. If they see a home that has no cars in the driveway and is empty most of the day, well, there is potential there. You can rely on the sad reality that most Americans take ZERO precautions when attempting to deter criminals.

This means that every step you take to set up deterrents is going to put your home lower and lower on the list of desirable properties in your neighborhood for criminals. It will be tiny tweaks here and there that make your home safer. You could argue that building giant walls around the home might be too much of a deterrent.

It is possible to fortify your home overly. The right number of deterrents puts criminals off, but a serious obstacle piques their interest and makes them wonder, *what are they protecting in there?* The perception might be something valuable is hiding behind those bars and walls.

Dogs

These little creatures have been the human alarm system for thousands of years. They are the best. Though I have snuck up on my dogs in the dark of night while they were sleeping, if someone starts banging at your door at night, you will know it. Dogs give you a heads up, but they also just deter. If a criminal has a choice between the quite empty home and the home with a dog, it is a no brainer!

Security System

A quality security system can act as a deterrent. Good criminals will know how to work around it, but you should broadcast it if you have a good system, so the bad guys know.

Secure Windows

The easier it is to get in, the more likely people will get in. If a bad guy has to rattle and wrench at the windows, they run the risk of being seen or waking up the homeowner.

Good Lighting

Motion lights and floodlights are great ways to keep your doors visible. High visibility at the front and back doors makes criminals nervous. They do not want to be seen coming or going. Bright lights will keep them from picking your home.

Gates

If they can walk right up to your home without hopping fences or opening gates, that's a good day for a criminal. A gate is another level of deterrent.

Clear and Open Yards

Yards that are filled with bushes, trees, and junk will provide a criminal with all kinds of options. The more hiding spots they have on the way to your side window or backdoor, the more likely they are to target your home.

Cars in Driveway

Does someone work from home? If there is a car in the drive and someone milling about at all times, then criminals are just going to keep on walking by. The last thing most criminals want is any interaction with the human element. Even if you take 2-3 of these deterrents and focus on them, you will make your home more of a sanctuary. You will have a home that is completely unappealing to society's worst elements, and that is precisely where you want to be.

Fortifying Your Home

When it comes to fortifying the home, you can wade into the realm of fantasy if you aren't careful. You could find yourself trying to turn your home into a bunker from which you can fight a war. That is the wrong train of thought. If you do not believe me, I want you to answer one simple question.

Who in Your Home is an Acceptable Casualty?

In military operations, there is a metric known as acceptable casualties. It is expected that there will be casualties in a military engagement. Suppose there aren't any on that particular mission, well, great! However, they plan on losing people on certain missions. When you start looking at yourself as more of a soldier than a spouse and parent, that is a problem.

The answer to the question is that your family unit is not prepared to lose anyone. Therefore, you cannot operate as a force that is prepared to take and return gunfire. If you are pretending like that is an option, then you are insane. For this reason, above all, you should not plan on fortifying your home for war. We will talk about what the better option is in the next section.

If you are dead set on fortification, I would say that improving doors and windows can go a long way. Most doors are weak. Locks are easy to bypass, and hinges can be removed with a good crowbar. A strong metal door can go a long way, and a company called Door Armor will help you fortify all the susceptible areas on your doors.

You can replace locks on windows and replace old windows. You can even install bulletproof glass on your windows too! This means that a typical smash-and-grab gets a lot harder for the average criminal.

Think of fortification as less about shooting the AR15 from behind sandbags and more about breaking the will of people who want to get into your home. This sounds complex and arduous, but to be honest, most people aren't that strong-willed. Criminals are professional opportunists, and the opportunity is fleeting. The right moment to take a home comes and goes quickly.

If your locks are fortified and your windows do not break, you will not only be alerted, but the criminals will also run off because they realize the operation has been compromised. Focus on breaking the will of the criminal from afar.

THE IMPORTANCE OF ESTABLISHING A DEFENSIVE PERIMETER

In an SHTF situation, the basic criminal will not be your only threat. Threats will be more common, and attacks will be more severe. So, you should go above and beyond the idea of home security. Home security is designed to address threats that can be handled at the household level. SHTF is not a situation that should be handled by a single household. SHTF is a community or a neighborhood problem.

The scope of your security expands, and you find yourself trying to understand how not just to keep your home safe but how do you keep a whole neighborhood safe. The great news is the same principles apply. You can detect, deter, and defend a community by using a simple defensive perimeter.

Creating your Community Boundary

To execute a community-wide defensive perimeter, you first have to define the boundary. It is up to you, in most cases, to determine the borders of your neighborhood. You need a reliable map of your community to start this process. This map will give you all the clues you need to define the perimeter in your neighborhood.

Some easy identifiers can help you establish that perimeter. Let's look at some of those identifiers.

Main Roads

Main roads need to be cut off. You need to set up a perimeter off the main roads. There is too much trouble that can occur there.

Access

Access to your perimeter is essential. People need to be able to easily walk that perimeter and identify and eliminate threats quickly and effectively.

Ability to Defend

These areas should also be easy to defend. You should have cover and high ground all along your perimeter. You will need a topographic map for this.

Vantage Points

Vantage points are designed to give those who are monitoring the perimeter a means of using optics or their eyes to see threats coming from a long way away. This is the most crucial part because you do not want to meet a threat with one person. You want to meet a threat with a force that deters them first.

Once you have established this defensive perimeter, you need to calculate how many patrolled positions are necessary to make this perimeter effective. You also need to know how many people are required to operate each position.

A perimeter position is not one person per position. Instead, it is more like one position equals four people. These people have to go home. Eventually, they have to eat and use the bathroom. So, you need multiple people to man each position. If you have five defensive positions along your perimeter, that could mean that you need 20 people in total to man those positions! That's a lot of people!

As this endeavor will require so many people, a level of democracy will have to go into your plans. You can be the architect of the perimeter and maybe even have some gear that can be handed out amongst people in your group. However, you are going to have a lot of nuances to discuss with 20 people who are working a defensive perimeter in your community. So, leave some things open for interpretation.

Define the perimeter, establish a communications method, and ensure that everyone understands the importance of this. From there, your community must have their say. You might hate it, but you need to hear them out.

Do Not Fight a War From Your Porch

Imagine the world has been turned completely upside down, and there is chaos in the streets. Imagine that there was no plan to get things back under control, and you and yours are huddled in your home, hoping to avoid the chaos. Maybe you have taken the steps we mentioned in previous chapters, and you were somewhat prepared.

In the dark of night, you are woken by a rumble outside of your home. You hop up out of bed. Your head is foggy, and you are quickly trying to wake up. Out the window, you see so many lights. When you part the blinds of your bedroom window, you see four pickup trucks lined up outside of your home, and there are multiple men, armed men, hopping out of the trucks and spreading out through your community.

What do You do Next?

If you find yourself in a situation like this, your security protocols have failed drastically. You cannot fight a war from your porch because you have everything to lose, and the men on the trucks can just go wild. You put your family at risk, you put your community at risk, and your preps, too! These guys are here for what you have. That could be food, ammo, or even people!

Your greatest motivation in neighborhood security is to ensure this never happens. Even if it requires that you create checkpoints and barriers to get into your neighborhood, it is well worth it. Even if you drop trees and park cars to assure that driving into your community is impossible, that is what must be done to avoid fighting a battle from your porch.

Once the bad guys are inside your community, you are going to lose a lot of people. You will have to retreat or create a new formation using radios while you are under attack. Unless you practice this in your community through drills, it is highly unlikely that it will ever happen. It is more likely the bad guys will move through your community, take everything, and kill the people.

This is the importance of security. This is the reason you need firearms and plans to ensure you stop threats at the perimeter of your community. This one scenario is why you live by the three Ds of security.

A NOTE ON FIREARMS

It is easy to go deep and get side-tracked on the path of developing your prepper arsenal. For some, this is most of the fun. You will need firearms if you are going to survive an actual SHTF situation in the suburbs. There is no getting around this part of the game. If the police are gone, and the bad guys have guns, you only have one option.

Let me save you a bunch of time and some arguments by giving you the very best loadout for new preppers and maybe all preppers. You might expect to see something like an AR15 or an AK47 on my list. However, those guns do not even make the top 3. You can accomplish everything you need to, from security to food procurement with three guns. These three guns are going to make your life much easier and will be weapons you use regularly. These firearms have been my go-to for many reasons.

- Ease of use
- Plentiful Ammo
- Affordable
- Effective

9MM Semi-Automatic Handgun

9mm ammunition is some of the most highly distributed in the nation. The gun itself has plenty of stopping power, and most have a minimal kick for a new shooter. These guns can be had for under $300.

The 9mm is also a great weapon to be carried daily. Having a firearm on your person each day is the best way to ensure your safety. As society degrades and violence becomes more prevalent in our streets, you will want a cheap and effective weapon at your side, just in case.

12 Gauge Shotgun

You can put a different sized shot through your 12 gauge, and all will be devastating to your prey. This is a great hunting weapon and maybe the best home defense weapon on the market.

Ammo for your 12 gauge is cheap and easy to get. A cheap shotgun is only going to run you about $200 bucks.

.117 Pump Air Rifle

You could argue about having a powerful hunting rifle, or you could talk about having a .22 rifle over an air rifle.

The air rifle is such an excellent option for preppers because you can use it for hunting small game, you can kill varmints and animals that are eating up your garden. If you buy the right model, this gun can even deter people because they look pretty similar to real rifles to the untrained eye.

However, the big win with the air rifle comes through ammo. Even though a .22 long rifle is cheap ammo, you cannot beat a 500 count for under $20. These guns are also very affordable, and most are around $100 for a good model.

KEY CHAPTER CONCEPTS:

- Understand the 3 D's of security.
- Focus your efforts on deterrents.
- Establish a community perimeter.
- Do not plan on fighting a war from your front porch.
- Consider the right firearms for you and your family.

7

ESSENTIAL #5 ENERGY

ARE YOU READY TO SURVIVE OFF-GRID?

Our reliance on things like clean running water and limitless electricity has made American life an absolute dream. It is a dream we often take for granted until one of these services is shut off. When the power goes out, most people are so angry that their electricity party has come to an end.

We are mostly incapable of sitting quietly and enjoying the power loss. For most of us, these outages last hours at the most.

Have you ever contemplated what life might be like if the electricity went off and never came back on? Are you prepared for that? You might not even realize it, but electricity is responsible for so many things.

- Electric Stoves
- Fridges
- Hospitals
- Communications
- Pumping Gas
- Heating
- Air Conditioning
- Entertainment
- Cell Phones

Grid Down Causes

So, how on earth could we find ourselves in this situation? What would it take to bring down the grid forever?

Unfortunately, it is not as complicated as you might assume. The American power grid is mostly unprotected, hard to repair, and susceptible to several attacks and even natural threats.

Electromagnetic Pulse (EMP)

Since the nuclear detonation near Bikini Island, we understand an EMP's potential to do serious damage to an electrical grid. The power of atomic bombs in the 40s was much different than today.

How Different?

The Fat Man that was dropped on Japan was a 21-kiloton bomb. The Castle Bravo, which is our most powerful known modern nuclear weapon, is a 15-megaton bomb.

The output difference is massive, and the results are terrifying. The fallout is far more expansive, and a weapon of this size could trigger an enormous EMP.

A high-altitude detonation over the central US would create an EMP capable of crippling our three main power grids. This would effectively send us back to the 1800s.

However, humankind is not the only threat when it comes to an EMP. Our life-giving sun has more than enough power to put the lights out on us with just a single burp of plasma. You see, the sun releases solar flares that occur when the sun's magnetic field is disrupted. The lines twist and snap, releasing a massive flare.

If a solar flare of the right size were to hit the planet, it would cause a worldwide blackout. One of the right size passed through our orbit, but we weren't at that point in our revolution. Many believe it is only a matter of time.

Terrorism

One of the best ways for a terrorist group to stop the United States in their tracks would be to launch a coordinated attack on one or more of the nation's major electrical grids. These three grids are massive and hard to repair and replace.

Most of the components come from China, so if we were to find ourselves at odds with that nation, we could have real trouble.

Human Resources

Every day some men and women go to work with the sole purpose of keeping your lights on. That is an astounding thing when you think about it.

If we were to face an event that disrupted their ability to go to work and operate the power stations, there could be no power without the people who make it possible each day. This type of event could be a pandemic that makes too many workers sick, or it could come from civil unrest that locks people in their homes to avoid violence. If human resources are affected, then our electricity will be shut off.

Backup Power Options

Just because the power grid goes down does not necessarily mean you and yours must be out of power. Thanks to the motivation to fuel our planet with cleaner energies, we have been exploring many backup power options or even off-grid power.

There are plenty of people in this nation who live strictly off-grid and are not even tethered to the power grid or the water system. If you aren't planning on moving to an off-grid homestead anytime soon, you can still affect your response to short- and long-term power outages.

Portable Gas Generators

The portable gas generator is probably the most affordable and most effective means of powering up the home during an outage. Portable gas generators can be small systems that you can carry or larger systems on wheels.

For years, we have depended on a 5500-watt system in power outages. These give us the ability to turn on lights, television, and entertainment, keep the fridge going, and even power some fans in the summer. It is more than enough power to get through a short-term power outage.

The problem with a reliance on gasoline is that we are only capable of storing so much. This means you will eventually run out of gas in a long-term scenario.

Whole House Generators

The next level of generating electricity is a whole house generator that is often tapped into a natural gas flow. These generators are built into your home and will click on when the power goes out. People love these larger generators because they just keep normalcy rolling even when others are out of power.

The whole house generator is a serious investment and can cost tens of thousands of dollars to install.

In an SHTF situation, the whole house generator could make you a target if you have all your lights on and HVAC (heating, ventilation, and air conditioning) running while the collapsing world around you is struggling.

Solar Panels

Solar power is a very interesting backup power solution. Harnessing the power of the sun just makes good sense. Solar panels can be pieced together over time, or you can go with a professional company to outfit your home.

The solar panels themselves are not affected by an electromagnetic pulse. However, some of the components will be. Safely storing backup components will give you the ability to generate power even after an EMP.

Solar panels cost roughly $1 per watt of energy generated, and DIY is not as hard as you might think. The most critical consideration in all of this is to ensure you get enough sun to power the batteries in your system day after day.

Wind Power

Wind power is another option when it comes to backup power. However, a wind power system can only really generate power if you have plenty of fans and space, like a wind farm, or if you live in a place that is essentially windy all the time.

The wind pushes the rotating blades, and the electricity generated is stored in batteries. The trouble comes when the wind dies down. A wind power system is ineffective if you do not have consistent wind to blow those turbines or turbines high up enough to capture the wind above you.

SHORT TERM POWER OUTAGE PREPAREDNESS

(Up to one month with the expectation that power is coming back on)

In a short-term power outage, you are going to have issues, but they will be nothing like a long-term power outage. Still, you will want to have several plans and things in place to deal with the surprise short-term power outage.

Simple Tip:

Outdoor solar lights are a great option for home lighting during a power outage. The solar lights that sit in your driveway or on your fence posts can be brought inside to light your home in the short term. They are very useful for this purpose and save your candles and flashlight batteries.

Step 1: Blackout Kit

The blackout kit is a fundamental prep that all homes should have on hand. This is an immediate response kit that allows you to get lights into people's hands and get started determining why you are in the dark.

This kit sounds cool, but creating one can be very simple. You do not need a whole lot of high-tech equipment. Our blackout kit consists of:

- flashlights
- lanterns
- candles
- power banks
- emergency radio

With these items, we can light up the night, the home and also get information on weather in the area and other news about what might have caused the power outage if it wasn't weather-related.

Flashlights for the whole family, especially for small children, are particularly important to have in the blackout kit. This way, no one is afraid of the situation.

Step 2: Initiate Potential Backup Power Systems

Now that everyone has a means of lighting up their immediate area, you can start taking the next steps. One of the first things to consider is what you will do with backup power. This depends on the type of power outage you are experiencing. If you call your power company and they tell you that power will be back on in an hour or two, then you probably aren't going to drag out the generator.

However, if you have hours or days even, you might look to start up that backup power system.

Step 3: Charge

If you connect to a backup power option, you should initially consider any items that will be needed for the power outage duration. Ideally, the items you have on hand are already charged so that you will have some time, but you should make sure all things are charged up when you are running backup power. You could also use the power banks from your blackout kit to charge up items.

Step 4: Conserve

Backup power is what it is, and it should be conserved at all costs. If you are working off a solar battery, you want to be careful with how much power you drain off that battery.

Be sure that only the essentials are running and turn everything off when it is not in use. Things like fans and simple lights are easy to forget. If the power outage happens at night, you can fall asleep and leave them on overnight. Conservation can be hard with kids because they will want everything back to normal. Practicing having the power off for a few hours every couple of months will help them have a working experience if and when the real power outage occurs.

Step 5: Wait

With any short-term power outage, there is going to be time. You are going to have some time to chill out and play games or just connect as a family. These things are important. We rarely get time to play a board game or just talk without phones, television, and other interruptions.

You could also go out and eat or just enjoy the outdoors while you wait for the power to come back on. Looking up at the stars when the town has no lights on is a great way to bond with your children and family.

LONG TERM POWER OUTAGE PREPAREDNESS

(Anything over one month without assurance that power will return)

A long-term power outage is chaos. There is no getting around it. We have never witnessed a peaceful long-term power outage in a populated area. It just does not happen. These two things are night and day.

The reality is, most people are not prepared to deal with a long-term power outage. They do not have the food, fuel, or even extra money stored up to pay bills and take care of day-to-day life. For a long-term power outage, you need to look at the situation much differently than being out of power for a week.

When I say long-term, I am talking about a situation in which the power will be out for a month or more! Maybe the power will never come back on again, and we talked about how that could happen at the beginning of the chapter. In a situation like this, you have to make hard decisions. The first and most important of which is whether you are going to stick this power outage out at home or if you are going to evacuate or even bug out until the power returns.

Planning to bug in or stay home during a long-term power outage makes a lot of sense because you will have all of your preps on hand. You will have neighbors around you, and you will be close to family.

By leaving for a bugout location, you are cutting yourself off from some of these benefits. However, you might also be getting away from any serious threats. If you are in a big crowded city, then you need to get away from that place in a long-term power outage. There are just not enough resources to sustain everyone, and things will get ugly in a hurry.

Most of us will choose to bug in and face this grid-down scenario with the preps that we have stored at home and the skills we have developed. Make no mistake about it. The grid-down scenario is among the most dangerous of all disasters.

There will be many things for you to address, and this means that an off-grid emergency deserves a written emergency response plan. Do not try to juggle all the different changes and needs on instinct. You are preparing, right? To best execute, you should have a full-scale off-grid plan.

This plan should start by gathering the family at your chosen location. No matter what time of the day or night it is, you need to get everyone home or to a secure site. The best way to draw this plan up is to create your plan for the middle of a workday. If you are at work, your kids are at school, and your spouse is at work, how do you get home and get everyone to safety.

It all starts with having a location for everyone to meetup. Remember, most grid-down situations are going to affect your ability to communicate drastically. Cell phones will either not work, or networks will be entirely blocked as the mass of people panic and begin to understand what is happening.

Your plan to rally the family at a disclosed location will need to happen with or without communications. This is not that big of a hurdle if everyone in your family understands where they will meet.

If you have young children, the best place to meet is going to be at their school. If you have one young child and one older but not old enough to walk to your younger child's school, parents should know exactly which child to pick up and go right home. This is a simple process, but if you are confused, or you do not have a plan, then it will make things much worse.

From the moment your family is gathered together, your plan becomes very personal. I cannot tell you how to build out your off-grid preparedness plan. All I can say is that all of your preps will help you survive a grid down scenario much better than leaving them behind for another location. If you can stay home and weather the storm, do that!

Essential Items in a Power Outage

There are many items that you will need to consider in a power outage. Things like hygiene, food preparation, security, and sanitation are some of the biggest ones. Let's look at a list of essentials for which you will likely need to find alternatives.

Alternative Lighting:

- Blackout Kit
- Candles
- Rechargeable Solar Lights
- Flashlights
- Headlamps
- Oil Lamps
- Natural Lighting
- Changing your sleep patterns (go to bed when the sun goes down)

Alternative Cooking:

Most stoves are electric, so you need a plan for off-grid cooking. The following are a list of many alternatives to electric cooking:

- Propane Camping Stoves
- Wood Burning Stove
- Outdoor Grills
- Outdoor Wood Fired Pizza Oven
- Alcohol Stove
- Rocket Stove
- Butane
- Propane
- Pressure Cookers (Fuel Conservation)
- Solar Ovens

Alternative Heating:

- Wood Burning Heaters
- Electric Space Heaters
- Fireplace
- Propane Heater
- Alcohol Heater

Is it a Long Term or Short-Term Power Outage?

One of the most important parts of energy preparedness is your ability to discern between a short-term power outage and a full-scale EMP attack. As you can tell, these two are very different. The short-term power outage is something we all efficiently manage regularly, while the EMP is a world-changing event that will lead to many people's death.

Obviously, the quicker you can discern between the two, the faster you will react, and the more effective you will be. The good news is that you can take some quite simple steps to tell whether or not you are experiencing an EMP. Because of the drastic effect it has on our power grid. You can tell in just a few minutes if you know what you are looking for.

Step 1: Check your lights and breakers. Ensure the power to your home is completely out.

Step 2: Check your vehicle. All modern vehicles are controlled through computers and electronics. These will be disabled following an EMP. Unless you have an old car, your car will be inoperable.

Step 3: Check your phone. Your phone will also be dead following an EMP.

Step 4: To avoid a potentially embarrassing reaction, check with your neighbor. If they are suffering from the same situation with phone, power, and car. You are facing an EMP.

Step 5: Check the skyline, highways, or distant lights at night. The EMP causes massive power surges, and these power surges will cause fires. You should see no lights but the distant glow of a fire.

If you are facing an EMP, you have to understand that it will be one of the toughest survival challenges to face.

This is the very worst-case scenario when it comes to emergency preparedness.

Creating a simple blackout kit will help you deal with the majority of blackouts that you and your family face. You should also consider some alternative power sources for longer-term blackouts that follow things like hurricanes and other natural disasters.

If you are genuinely interested in beating the power outage, then you should be on a mission to slowly and thoughtfully remove yourself from the power grid. You might be able to achieve this solely through solar power. It might take a combination of renewable energies to pull this off and a change of your lifestyle.

No matter your approach to dealing with energy preparedness, you will need to collect stored alternatives for cooking, light, electricity, a blackout kit, and a long-term power outage plan. Be sure you can gather the family in a no comms grid-down scenario, and you will be starting in the right place.

KEY CHAPTER CONCEPTS:

- There are many ways that we can lose power – some short-term, some long-term.
- Consider the solar and backup gas-powered generators as ways of turning the power back on.

- Be prepared with some off-grid, no electricity preps to help you cook, clean, and have fun in a power outage.

8

ESSENTIAL #6 HYGIENE

ARE YOU READY TO STAY CLEAN AND DEAL WITH YOUR FAMILY'S WASTE?

What is the number one killer in SHTF? Do you fear the biker gangs or the gang leaders or the bands of desperate roving people? Thanks to Hollywood and works of fiction, we assume the human threat is the greatest in SHTF. We prepare because we do not want our lives to end at the wrong end of a knife or a gun barrel.

In reality, you are far more likely to be taken out by an infection or illness. Thanks to modern medicine and easy access to clean water, we rarely concern ourselves with infection. If you do away with waste management and good personal hygiene, suddenly, those old concerns our ancestors had can come roaring back. Just by losing access to clean water, you start a chain reaction of all kinds of problems.

You and yours will need an inventory of personal hygiene items. You will also need the means to deal with your waste and likely agree with neighbors that they will do the same with their waste, or else all your work will be in vain.

If trash is allowed to pile up all over your town or community, remember trash collectors will not be coming each week during SHTF, you will eventually have trash all over the streets, and next will come disease-causing pests. Now you have to worry about dealing with diseases and other issues that go along with pests. One of the big ones is how they get into your home and break into your food storage or pantry.

THE 6 KEY AREAS TO SANITATION

Personal Sanitation

We have come a long way in terms of personal hygiene. Did you know there was a time, not that long ago, when humans fought the scourge of fleas and lice? Not fleas on their dogs but on themselves. It was so bad that people in medieval times chose to lay their clothes over the privy chamber or toilet so that the fumes would delouse and de-flea their clothing!

Modern bathing practices and daily hygiene have made this a non-issue for most people in America. However, we rely on a consistent stream of clean water and access to several resources that keep us clean and free from infection. If you are going to build a cache of personal sanitization items, you are going to want to keep a few things on hand at all times.

- Single-Use Hygiene Items
- Essential Oils
- Waste Collection

Baby wipes, nitrile gloves, toilet paper, and trash bags are all going to be essential when it comes to storing single-use items. You could also include hand sanitizer.

Essential oils are a great ally in any personal hygiene program. Many people will store up toothpaste and deodorant as part of their hygiene preps. However, if these items were to become scarce, you can do a lot of things with essential oils, baking soda, and salt.

Simple Toothpaste

Materials:

- 1/2 Cup of Baking Soda
- 10 Drops of Mint Essential Oil
- 1 TSP of Salt

Method:

The method is quite simple for making this. All you do is mix the ingredients. You can add more or less mint depending on your personal preferences.

Simple Deodorant

Materials:

- 4 TBSP of Arrowroot
- 1 TBSP of Baking Soda
- 10 Drops of Lavender Oil

Method:

These items can be mixed and used under your arms, or you can add a half cup of witch hazel and use this as a spray-on.

As you can see, there are some aspects of personal hygiene preparedness that can be made and not bought. It is better to have the skills to make these items rather than just rely on someone else to make them, and you have access to them. There could come a time where the toothpaste isn't available anymore.

When it comes to building your cache of single-use items, there is one method that works best. Simply buy yourself a large bin, trash can, or some other large lidded container. Whenever you are out shopping, buy yourself an extra pack of toilet paper, a bar of soap, or some sanitary wipes. Just start piling these into that one large bin, and over six months, you will be packed, deep, with soap, toilet paper, and other single-use hygiene items.

Showering and Bathing

In many ways, we can turn back to the water section when it comes to showering and bathing. The water catchment becomes particularly important to personal hygiene. This is another reason why I recommend storing 3 gallons of water per person per day rather than just 1 gallon.

Not only will you want to have access to that water, but you may even want to invest in some sort of backup shower system. If you have plumbing knowledge, you could pipe water into your existing shower pipes.

If you aren't into that, you should invest in a simple camping shower system. They sell a bunch of these of differing varieties. A simple camping shower can feel amazing if you have not had a full-body wash in several days. There is no getting around the fact that you need to clean your body from time to time.

Between showers, you might also look to wipe yourself down for a more straightforward cleaning solution. There is a company called Combat One that makes incredible wipes that contain antibacterial colloidal silver. These wipes can be used to clean your entire body. Having some kind of wipe in an SHTF situation will be very important to cleanliness.

Bathing will likely dominate, and a shower will be a rare occurrence. Bathing in SHTF means transporting large amounts of water from your water reserves to your bath-tub. Be sure you have some large pots or totes to pull that off.

Human Waste Disposal

Human waste disposal is something we have been doing since the Romans! While it was hardly as polished as our systems today, it was well understood that we could not live amongst our filth. When the water stops running or the toilets back up, do you have a game plan for dealing with human waste?

If your game plan is to dig catholes, or 6-inch-deep holes in the ground, to manage waste, I would encourage you to expand on that thought. While catholes can be useful on camping trips and missions, the area around your home should not be riddled with cat holes and human waste. You also have to consider the winter and how digging holes and using the bathroom out in the open will work. It won't!

The good news is there are many alternatives when it comes to dealing with human waste disposal. When it comes to these kinds of challenges, I always look to the communities of people who already live off-grid and are doing these things daily.

What would be perfect is if you could turn your waste into food for your gardens and plants? Well, that is precisely what some off-grid homesteaders do using composting toilets. These small toilets are used in the process of making something dubbed "humanure." While our feces are not safe like goat or horse, they can be made so. It has to go through its composting process.

Compost toilets have a small crank handle that is turned after each use to start this process. You can have a larger sawdust and waste system outside the home that turns the waste into something usable.

You could also dig and build an outhouse. These can be highly effective and shelter you while using the bathroom. The digging in your area should be done with the local restrictions in mind. There are lots of rules about how deep and how far away from water they should be. Beyond the hole, the outhouse is a simple build to encase the person using it and allow for ventilation.

Another very simple setup is to use a simple bucket with a fashioned toilet seat. You can start by layering peat and sawdust at the bottom of the 5-gallon bucket. Between uses, you cover the waste completely with peat and sawdust. When full, this mix will go to a larger pile outside, which could be turned into humanure.

Simple Handwashing Station

Human feces are very dangerous. Do you know that our intestinal tract is full of bacteria like salmonella, E. Coli, viruses, and other pathogens? If allowed to hang around, these bacteria will grow and become extremely dangerous to the people exposed to them. This exposure will happen when you use toilet paper. To mitigate the risks, we need to be prepared to set up a simple hand washing station.

Here are the Items You Will Need to Set up Your Simple Handwashing Station:

- Liquid Soap
- Water Source (Raised rain barrel can be great for this)
- Single-Use Paper Towels
- Hand Sanitizer
- Trash Can

If you can manage human waste and clean your hands and arms when dealing with that waste, you will keep disease and infection at bay. This is a fundamental concept because we do not consider it, but we will all have to consider it in an SHTF situation.

Without proper human waste management, we will contaminate the local water resource and bring pests and disease into our living areas.

Solid Waste Disposal

Solid waste disposal is probably the most underappreciated service in the world. This is something that happens every week to keep our streets and waterways clean. Most Americans have no idea how much waste they produce. A family of 4 produces roughly a full trash bag of waste each day, from packaging to food waste, to cleaning waste.

Our waste is not only collected from our homes, but it is taken far away and stored in a variety of ways to keep it out of our view. It is a weird system because we bury most of our trash, and some we just throw in lots outside of town.

If not for the weekly trash collection, our streets would be piled high with solid waste. We are a packaged society. With the influx of online shopping, we are disposing of even more packaging at the residential level.

You need to have a plan to deal with solid waste in a suburban SHTF situation, and your plan better include others. The suburbs are very different from living in the country. In the country, you can manage your trash the way you like and not have to worry about your neighbor a mile down the road.

However, in the suburbs, your neighbors' trash will be your trash in a hurry. All that goes along with your neighbor's trash will also be yours. Trash piles will bring pests, it will blow into your yard, and eventually, you will have a severe health hazard in your community.

Lifestyle Changes for Managing Solid Waste

You can limit your waste both in your home and in your community by changing your lifestyle and how you manage solid waste. You can save all kinds of space in your garbage bags when you start composting food waste. We waste a lot of food and parts of food. Rinds, moldy bread, and out of date produce make up a large portion of waste. This stuff can be turned into plant food! Do not miss out on this.

Plastic and glass containers can go a long way. We often throw those glass containers away or put them in recycling. You can also just turn those pickle jars into drinking glasses! You can store nuts and bolts in them or whatever else. These are great little containers. Hard plastic containers can be reused as well. Remember, your ability to reuse things in an SHTF situation will benefit you and your family!

Packaging that cannot be reused needs to be broken down, so it takes up the least amount of space possible. Breaking down packaging gives you the ability to fit more into a smaller area. Crushing things like cans and breaking down cardboard and plastic containers goes a long way. However, you will eventually have to do something with this garbage. You are likely going to have to burn some of your garbage on a weekly basis. This is where you might consider a community setup rather than a personal one. If you have a place where neighbors can lug their trash and burn it, you will likely have less of a pile-up and residual pest problem.

Managing trash and solid waste in suburbia will have to be a joint effort, or you will be overrun. The trash is going to pile up extremely fast. We do not realize what a burden our waste management teams shoulder for the public.

Laundry, Cleaning, Washing

Washing up after meals and cleaning clothes is not something that will go away with an uncivil society. You will still need to clean up after meals, and clothes will still need to be washed, folded, and put away. The difference is you will not have a dishwasher to load or a washing machine to unload. Things could get incredibly difficult when it comes to clothes and dishes.

A simple stockpile of scrubbing pads, dish soap, and laundry detergent will go a long way when handling these washing duties in a crisis. You can also add things like Borax and baking soda to this stockpile as these are multi-purpose substances that can be used for cleaning, pest control, and even personal hygiene purposes.

In terms of dishes, you could also invest in disposable utensils, plates, and cups, but just remember, while this eliminates a cleaning problem, it creates a waste problem.

Growing Hygiene

While most people do not consider it, a few plants can be grown to help with personal hygiene. The beauty of these plants is that you can save the seeds and create your own little hygiene factory year over year. We are going to focus on two plants in particular and a collection of herbs.

Loofah

The loofah is a remarkably interesting squash that has found its way into the showers of many Americans. While most people think of squash as something you would use in the sauté pan, the loofah is dried and becomes a means of scrubbing your skin. Cloth will be precious, so having the loofah as an option to clean your body and even scrub surfaces in the home is invaluable. Loofahs are also prolific growers, though they do take up a good amount of garden space.

Licorice

We are all familiar with the taste of licorice root. It has been used to cure stomach upset over the ages. The root is very fibrous, and it can be used as a toothbrush. The end can be chewed to break apart the fibers, which will act as bristles, and the licorice scent and oils will help kill bacteria and flavor your breath.

Fresh Herbs

Herbs are powerful and can add both aromatics and antibacterial properties. At the very least, I would recommend growing rosemary, lavender, and oregano. These all have a great fragrance and will affect bacterial growth and infection.

You can add these fresh herbs to soaps, tinctures, salves, and even the soap and deodorant recipes we mentioned above.

No suburban lot would be complete without an SHTF hygiene garden. You can expand on these ideas and look into things like soapnut and other soap alternatives. They are out there. We have only recently limited ourselves to bar soaps and gels, but for centuries, we have used several different methods for maintaining personal hygiene.

Off-Grid Cleaning Methods

We have only been filling dishwashers and loading washing machines for 110 years, but we have been washing clothes for a long, long time! At its most primitive, clothes were beaten with rocks, rubbed with abrasive sands, and washed in the river. Of course, those materials were much different than the materials that we use now. I do not think our polyester blend t-shirts would do well if we beat them with rocks.

The metal washboard carried us from the late 1800s until the wide adoption of electric washing machines, which happened long after their invention in 1907. Investing in a simple washboard as one of these off-grid cleaning methods is not the worst idea.

The washboard can be combined with a few larger buckets and a hand crank ringer. Hot water and soap or baking soda can be used in the first bucket to soak and wash the clothing before rinsing it in a second bucket of clean water. Clothes can then be wrung out and hung up to dry. This older system used three buckets most of the time—one with cleaner and the other two with clean water.

Modern Off-Grid Methods

A clean 5-gallon bucket and a clean plunger can be used to wash small loads of clothes. Your clothes can be soaked in hot water in the bucket, and then your plunger becomes the agitator of the washing system. It would help to have some type of wringer for this system as the clothes will be very wet when you pull them from the bucket.

The Laundry Pod is a larger and more efficient hand crank washing machine that works the same way as a salad spinner. You can agitate the clothes, water, and soap by hand and then spin it to wash and drain the water from the machine. These machines are also very affordable to purchase and store for that SHTF moment where you still need to get the clothes washed.

Washing clothes and dishes is something you will be doing. No matter how terrible the world outside your four walls looks, you are going to need clean clothes to wear and clean plates and cups to eat and drink from to keep the pests at bay.

PEST CONTROL

Pest control will become a crucial issue in SHTF. The general public has no idea how much goes into keeping local pest populations at bay. There is a massive amount of land and water management that goes into simply dealing with mosquito populations. Your city is likely spraying chemicals, too, just to keep these monsters from annoying the population.

That said, you will be less worried about biting mosquitoes and more concerned about the mice and rats that are threatening your food supply. Remember, in an SHTF situation, trash collection is not going to be happening. While you might have a plan to deal with trash, your neighbors may not. This means you will have serious problems with pests of all sizes.

The good news: pest control is an industry. Pests have been widely studied, and mitigation strategies are well known. There is a pest control triangle that is very similar to the fire triangle. If you can affect all sides of this triangle, you will be able to keep pests at bay.

For any Pest Population to Exist, It Only Needs Three Things:

- Food
- Water
- Harborage (a place to nest)

There are many ways that you can affect all of these parts of the pest triangle. The first is to look around your home for leaks and water sources. It only takes a small but reliable runoff to satisfy the needs of small pests like mice and even rats. Simple drainage and filling of holes can eliminate pools of standing water around your home.

These creatures will wreak havoc on your food pantry and food supply if they make a home in your walls and roofing. Once they find their way into the home, they will find the food. If your food is left open and easy to access, things just get better for pests.

Storing food high on shelves and in food-safe containers can go a long way. If you find you have a pest problem, it might also benefit you to store food in jars and Tupperware containers rather than flimsy packaging that can be easily chewed through.

While your pantry is a large food source, pests are often brought to a property because of food access outside the home first. This could be the food in your chicken coop or the area around your trash cans. Cleanliness outside your home is step one. Storing pet and livestock feed in closed containers is vital. Pests love dog food!

Deny them the food, and they will have no desire to learn more about your home. Pest control is a lot like security in that way.

Harborage is another problem that derives from your ability to keep a clean home and garage. Your yard is part of this equation too. Animals use all kinds of things to build their homes. If you look at the average bird nest, you will see that it is composed of all types of things like string, plastic, ribbon, and whatever else the birds can find. If items are unorganized or scattered and areas under decks and sheds are left open, animals will use these materials and these locations to build their homes. Then they can spend more time exploring your home for water and food sources.

Pest control starts with a simple inspection of your home to see if you are contributing to the pest triangle in any way. However, you will need some items on hand if you do find cracks or holes in your foundation, flooring, or other entry points. Denial of entry is huge when it comes to managing pest populations.

- 2-inch lumber for drilling over holes under the home
- Epoxy for filling small gaps (mice will eat through caulk)

- Steel Scrub Pads for plugging smaller holes

If you find that you have an infestation during an SHTF situation, you will need some tools to manage that as well. Most people are queasy about dealing with pests and poisons, but you are going to need to keep your options open as these pests will bring disease and damage to your home and food supply.

- Outdoor Poison Bait
- Indoor Killing Traps
- Small Indoor Poison Stations

The use of poison is dangerous, but it must be available to you. The poison baits used in modern traps are designed to be eaten and scattered. These poisons are not only ingested but are also taken back to dens where the pests live. There, the poison can kill the den and all the pests too.

These same poisons will affect your family. So, be incredibly careful about where you store them, and be sure to check them each day. Do not leave them around open food as the pests could first take the poison before jumping into your food and spreading the poison. If you cannot keep the pests outside of your home, you will have to eradicate them.

KEY CHAPTER CONCEPTS:

- Hygiene is one of the most overlooked preps of all.
- You can grow, store, and make many of the things you need to clean your home and yourself.
- Focus on solid waste and human waste. You need a plan for both of these!
- Have some pest control solutions in your storage plan.

9

IS EVERYONE READY?

TEACHING YOUR KIDS EMERGENCY PREPAREDNESS

From the time they can understand what you are saying, you can begin preparing your kids for emergencies. Children are born with an innate survival instinct. When they start walking, you might have trouble believing this because they will get themselves into so much trouble! That said, even babies understand that loud noises and unfamiliar faces can be a problem.

The earliest survival training that you undergo with your kids is to avoid strangers. The idea of 'not talking to strangers' is something we teach our youngest children in society. This is excellent training, and it allows your child to understand the genuine threats that exist in our world.

For some reason, we look at things like teaching kids about strangers and teaching them about inappropriate touching as good parenting. Still, if you teach your young child about self-defense or something like a fire or blackout response, you can be labeled as 'extreme'. To understand how to teach your kids about emergency preparedness, you must first decide what they need to know and stand by it.

Two years ago, if you told your co-workers that you were building a pandemic kit that was fully stocked with a teaching curriculum for your children because a pandemic could shut down schools and stores for an extended period, they would look at you funny. If you told them you were going to talk to your child about the potential of a pandemic in the future and how they might not be able to go to school, they might report you! Know your convictions and act from a position of planning and power, not fear.

At Home

The very basis of teaching kids' emergency preparedness is the creation of a safe place at home. The home must resonate with safety so that kids can grasp the concept of what a disaster or emergency might be like. Sadly, many kids exist in homes that are sheer chaos, and there is no safety for them. Your first and most important task is to provide your child with a safe home.

From there, you can turn them into whatever kind of bushcraft survivalist child you want! In the home, many different things can be learned. From locating specific emergency tools to running drills that are very important to preparedness, your kids should know where certain things are in the home and how to use them.

- Blackout kit
- Bugout bag
- Emergency communications
- First aid
- Emergency food
- Some type of age-appropriate weapon

Home training will make up most of your efforts, so you must take the time to speak to these concepts. Your kids not only need to know where these things are, but they should know how to put them to use. Make it a fun family bonding time instead of strict, regimented training. I cannot emphasize this enough.

Hidden Password Game

A fun game that you can play with your kids is the hidden password game. Create a signal word that you say, and the kids scatter and hide. Turn this into a game that you play regularly. Choose a word other than *hide* but one that is easily recognizable in the home.

Your kids will hide in the best spot they can find, and they will stay put. The password comes in next. This particular password is the only word that will get the kids out of hiding. Explain this at the beginning. Explain that no matter what Mom or Dad say, if they come out, they lose. You can only win the game if you come out when the password is uttered. Kids love this game, and they get a real kick out of scattering and hiding at a moment's notice.

This is excellent training for a break-in or other chaos outside of the home. If your kids are trained to hide at a moment's notice, then you can simply call out your signal word when someone strange walks up on your porch or if you hear something strange downstairs at night.

The password ensures that no one will be able to get them to come out unless they have the password.

THE HOME CULTURE

To do it well, preparedness has to become a lifestyle. If you can integrate things like outdoor adventure, fitness, gardening, archery, cooking, and other activities that promote self-reliance and independence, these things will begin to shape your life. Your kids will start to reflect your preparedness influence. These types of things will start to show up on your television, on your bookshelf, and maybe even in your kids' toy box. The younger you can get them engaged with three-step ahead thinking so that this becomes a normal way of life, the better.

While basic concepts like "stop, drop, and roll" and shelter-in-place can be taught, you want kids to be immersed in a culture of preparedness if you are truly planning for an SHTF situation in your neighborhood.

Another great benefit of living the kind of outdoorsy, homesteader lifestyle is that it introduces your children to real-life threats. If you spend time in the woods, you have to talk about bears. If you are raising chickens, you have to talk about predators. These conversations about predators and dangers will make bigger conversations during SHTF easier for kids to comprehend.

It is very easy to let your kids just drone on in front of screens today. Sometimes you have no control over what your kid is up to because you and your spouse are at work. However, if your home and your time together is spent productively and your home culture is built around being ready and spending time outside, your kids will take to prepping far more quickly.

Drills

At home, drills are one of the most important things you can do to ensure your family knows how to react in an emergency. If you are reading this book, then chances are you are more dedicated to preparedness than the other people in your home. However, you need to drill certain things in your home.

This is a rare annual or biannual practice that should include the entire family, no matter how much they huff and puff. Make it tough but exciting and make them think about their position and how they can both keep safe and help out.

Fire

The fire drill should be conducted at least on an annual basis and should block your main exit and entry points. In other words, you shouldn't be able to walk out of the front door during your fire drill. If a real fire allows for it, then it will be much easier, but do not count on using it.

A house fire isn't just going to burn in the halls and kitchens. If you wake up and find that access to your downstairs is limited, do you have an answer to that? Can you get out of your windows? Do you have some kind of ladder? How about getting pets out of the house?

Your fire drill should not be something everyone in your home is prepared for. You should spring it on the family and maybe discuss it ahead of time with your spouse. There will be a bit of chaos in a real fire, so you want the practice to include that element too. Fire drills at night can be effective, but most importantly, you just want to be sure that everyone knows how to react when the alarms start blaring, and you have to get out!

Shelter-in-Place

The next drill that you should run yearly is the shelter-in-place. This is important for bad thunderstorms, hurricanes, and tornadoes. It touches a bunch of issues, and that is why it is so important.

First, you need to identify your shelter-in-place locations correctly. Great spots are at the center of the home or beneath ground level.

- Basement
- Enclosed Space Under Steps
- Pantry
- Bathroom without Windows

Your shelter-in-place location will need to fit your entire family plus any animals that you want to shelter, too! Sometimes dogs have to be squeezed in tight.

There are also a few things that you are going to need inside your shelter-in-place location. Now, you could create a small bin of these items and leave them inside your shelter-in-place. That makes life much easier. At the very least, I like to have these things inside the room with my family.

- Lanterns or Flashlights
- Emergency Radio
- Kids Entertainment

- Food
- Water
- Small USB Powered Fan (You will get hot in that tight space!)

If you can fit everyone you hold dear and some light gear into this space, then you have yourself a great spot. Be sure you drill staying in there for at least 10 minutes together. This will highlight any pain points that need to be addressed. We remove the bottom shelf in our pantry as this adds dog room and gives them their little space away from our feet!

Break-In

While a home invasion is a much rarer occurrence than a fire or severe storm, it is one of the most traumatic experiences your family can experience. If you are not prepared, you can easily be left to the will of those who have done the breaking in.

Some thefts are focused around a quick smash and grab, while others can turn unbelievably violent. There seems to be an uptick in what I would call Robberies +, which are a combination of theft and assault or even murder.

For your children, they should know what steps to take when they hear something that goes bump in the night. The moves they make will be defined by you and yours, but they should be well aware. Things like secure, predetermined hiding places or heading to your bedroom are great ideas, but they need to be more than just ideas.

The triggers for this move could be anything from something that does not sound right at night, to a knock on the door, to seeing someone in the home. All of which can be terrifying for a child.

Away From Home

The fruits of your labor come into play when your children are away from home. What they do will help you understand whether or not they understand their role in preparedness. When I see polite and helpful children, I see some of the most important players in a disaster. Children like this are often calm and cool in high-stress scenarios. That is the key!

While you are out of the picture, there are some things that you can offer up to your child to ensure they are aware of and effective in a disaster or emergency. One of the simplest is to either have them memorize your address and phone numbers or to keep that info on their person. I prefer memory.

If they are carrying a backpack, there is no reason you cannot outfit them with a simple kit. Of course, you have to be clear with your kids that these items are not toys.

Let's Build a Quick Kit for Your Kids When They are Away From Home:

- Water Bottle
- Flashlight with backup batteries
- Emergency Whistle (good ones are incredibly loud)
- Simple Snack
- First-aid Kit
- Kids Poncho
- Small Book
- Small Wipes
- Cell Phone (big decision for most parents)

You can fit most of these items into a small pencil case so that it will be inconspicuous to anyone who looks in the bag or if your child takes it out to make room for something else.

In Disaster

Perhaps the most important lessons of all come amid disaster or emergency. Here you get to see your kids under the pressure of the unknown. This can make or break them depending on the child, their temperament, and their journey.

One of the greatest lessons anyone prepping to survive SHTF in Suburbia must take into consideration is that the first step is to remain calm. This is very hard for children because they can hardly stay calm on a car ride. When lights are blinking and phones beeping and radios making that crazy emergency alert noise, they get scared.

Remember, you are the living, breathing example of what a calm response to disasters should be. There are no words you can speak that will outweigh your actions in a crisis. You can tell them to remain calm until you are blue in the face, but if you are pulling out your hair, then they will see that and feed off it.

This is why it is so vital that you remain calm too! Disaster specific activities can be a great way to deal with things like storms and power outages. If you reserve a list of activities and games for only when disasters strike, your kids will get very excited when the power goes out, or the storms roll into town. You control the narrative on this, and you can either instill a sense of calm and fun or a sense of fear into them. I chose fun and calm every time!

Enjoying Life

It does not just have to be about preparing for a disaster. Developing survival skills and an understanding of self-reliance can be extremely rewarding. The great outdoors offers a multitude of opportunities.

Take your children into the wilderness, and not just as a vacation. Build the wonders of this world into your life. These are things like mountains, shorelines, highlands, meadows, and wetlands.

Hiking or fishing on the weekends will build something in your children that is tremendous and impossible to replicate. They will become familiar with the natural world; they will be immersed in fundamental survival skills like land navigation, and the lessons just build and build.

Swimming, hunting, and geocaching are other great activities that hook kids on the outdoors. Geocaching is the process of finding small hidden treasures that are placed around our nation and parts of the world by the geocaching community. Your job is simply to use coordinates and find the cache. Some of these caches contain small toys or items that can be traded. Others are simply a small stack of papers that you sign to prove you have found this particular cache. It is a great time and a wonderful way to teach your children about using their skills to search for something.

Our lust for life must be greater than our fear of death. This is not just a prepping lesson to teach your kids but one that will follow them all through life.

THE BIGGEST MISTAKE

If we are going to discuss who is ready and who is not, we need to talk about the single biggest mistake you can make as a person preparing for SHTF in Suburbia. A situation like this is going to cause widespread chaos and likely violence.

You cannot be the sole proprietor of survival knowledge at home. Since you are reading this, you must be the person who focuses most on prepping and survival. Without you, much of what needs to be done would not get done. However, if you make the mistake of holding all the info and not having others to help, you put your family and yourself at an even greater risk.

If you do not share your plans with kids and introduce them to the preparedness culture, they will be helpless in an SHTF situation. The weight of the moment will fall on you, and that might be too much to bear. Sure, you like to think that you will perform when it is all on the line. If your body fails or you get injured, your family will suffer, and no one will have the basic knowledge to get you back in the game.

Violence is rarely one-sided, and if someone attempts to break into your home, you could be wounded. The wound might cost you your life unless someone else in your family knows how to patch you up! Family members need to know how to stop people from bleeding to death!

It is much easier just to do all the work yourself. It is easier to mockup the plans and understand them. To gather the family around and be sure they understand them, well, that takes work. However, it will pay off when the time comes for you and yours to react.

Some family members can bristle at the idea of sitting down and learning about your emergency plans. Sometimes it is simply better to create an effective emergency response plan that they can turn to. The more training you can do as a family, the better. Do not forget, if you are already living an inherently independent lifestyle with a decent interest in the outdoors, that will go a long way too!

You cannot face down SHTF in suburbia by yourself. Nor should you try! Everyone will be safer and better off if they all do their part. Do not make the mistake of shouldering the full burden. It won't end well.

KEY CHAPTER CONCEPTS:

- Your home life will dictate much of your child's preparedness.
- Preparing them at home allows them to practice preparedness outside of the home.
- Include your kids in emergency drills.
- Do not make the mistake of keeping all the knowledge to yourself. Your family unit needs to be just that, a unit, a team! This is not a dictatorship.

10

THE BACKUP PLAN

WHEN BUGGING IN NEEDS TO BECOME BUGGING OUT

In the prepping community, we tend to toss around the word bugout far too liberally. It becomes more of a Band-Aid than an actual resource. That is a problem. Whenever things get too real, there are some preppers out there who just default to the bugout.

The bugout is a massive undertaking that requires investment, planning, and high-level execution to be most effective. It is not just a dot you put on a map and decide you will go there when everything gets squirrely. There are a lot of steps that go into bugging out, and if you are even remotely considering it, you should pay close attention to this chapter.

We will ask some fundamental questions about bugging out and set some very simple but necessary parameters for what you need to bug out effectively.

Can You Bug Out?

A question that many people do not ask themselves is, "Can I bug out?" Not everyone is capable of bugging out, and there are all kinds of reasons why that might be true for you too! There could be circumstances that keep you from bugging out that you have not even taken into consideration.

Your home is your greatest survival investment, remember? Simply emulating all of it at another location is going to be near impossible for most of us. So, you have to be very sure that bugging out is something you want to add to your bag of tricks.

What if you are severely disabled? Is bugging out something you want to deal with? Is it something you are capable of pulling off? There are some situations where you simply cannot bug out, or pulling it off will cause you tremendous pain or hardship.

What about the tens of thousands of Americans who care for elderly parents in their home? Could you figure out how to get your elderly parents to the bugout location? What if you were tasked with getting there on foot? A wheelchair through the woods is as ugly as it gets.

Things like medications, injuries, and illness all affect your ability to bug out. You have to sit down with your family and ask the questions. You have to walk through this bugout process and recognize your weakest links. Obesity is another problem in our nation, and many people who are morbidly obese struggle to walk to the mailbox, let alone head 10 miles down the road with a backpack on.

The good news is, you can overcome a lot if you take the time to plan. There is more to you than you think as long as you can be honest about your shortcomings.

There is an element of risk to bugging out and to everything we do in life. Even the most perfect bugout plan for two fit people, who are well-armed and prepared for success, can go bad. That said, there are some serious hindrances in people's way, and we have to be honest about what we are capable of because once you head out of the home, everything gets real!

Locations Before Bags

The biggest mistake we make when considering the bugout is to buy the bag and the contents before considering the location. It is a big problem! Imagine packing your bags for a vacation that you hadn't booked yet. You do not know where you are going or for how long, but you have your suitcases packed and ready to go. Do you need a bathing suit? Do you need sunscreen? Do you need a sweater?

This is how silly it is to pack your bugout bag before you even know where your bugout location is. Now, do not get down on yourself. You have been tricked into buying that bag and filling it up with gear. You see, the bugout is not just about being prepared and keeping people safe. No. The bugout is also about marketing and making money. There are all kinds of companies out there that are making money off writing posts, making videos, and scaring people into buying things. It is sad, but it is true.

This is how so many of us get conned into buying things we are not even sure we will need. For the most part, the things you buy will help in one aspect of preparedness or another. It is not a total waste. However, the idea that you have packed up the perfect bag without knowing where you are headed is kind of crazy.

So, Where do We Go?

The idea behind bugging out is that you must leave your home because you cannot live there anymore due to threats from the environment, people, or a lack of essential resources. Where you head should be the opposite. You should look for a place where you are safe, there are plenty of resources, and you can survive.

While many people like to believe they are going to bug out to the woods, that is a very tough way to live, and unless you are versed in long term camping, austere living, or something along those lines, you will not be able to last very long in the woods. However, I understand that many people have no other option.

Let's Look at Some Locations to Consider for a Safe Bug Out:

- Raw Land, you own
- Alternate Home
- Cabin
- RV
- Family-Owned Land
- State Park
- National Forest
- Family members home (most people do not consider this for an easy bug out!)

There are lots of options for bugout locations; just be sure you do not start trespassing as that could go bad. Do the easy stuff first. Talk to family about staying with them if you need to bug out. Chances are you have someone who lives in the country, and as long as you are going to do some work and not just be a drain on resources, they would like to have you. Once you have secured a location or a few, you need to start thinking about how you get there.

How do We Get There?

To get to your location, you are going to need to know the route. Everyone is going to need to know that route and how to get to the bugout location. This might be a route that travels highways or backroads.

For many people, once they have a route, they are good to go. They are going to jump in the vehicle and hit the road in an emergency. So, what happens when the road is blocked. What happens when that route is no longer an option?

Because of these situations that could arise, you need to have more than one route to get to your BOL. You could argue that you should have more than one BOL! However, that gets expensive, fast!

At the very least, you should have several routes to get to your BOL. Some of these should be on the road, and others should be on foot. Maybe include some bike routes as even more options. If you cannot get to your bugout location, then it isn't your bugout location anymore!

Avoid major roads when planning bugout routes. Avoid routes that take you over water. There are many obstacles on roads you travel every day that you might not consider until there is a disaster and you have to get through in a hurry.

You also need to consider what neighborhoods your bugout route is going to take you through. You want to avoid driving through or near rough neighborhoods in your city or town. You also need to understand that highly populated areas can suddenly turn into rough areas.

Craft yourself a few bugout routes that are going to get you where you need to be in times of emergency or disaster. Share these routes with your family, give them maps to carry in vehicles, and if it all comes apart, everyone will know where to go and how to get there.

Be prepared to go by vehicle and on foot. The locations and the means of travel will tell you everything you need to know about what you should pack in your bugout bag.

In this next section, we will delve deep into all the things you can store in your bugout bag and how to meet your survival needs while not putting hundreds of pounds on your back. The bugout bag can wear you down if you are not careful.

BUGOUT BAGS AND CONTENTS

Once you get an understanding of your bugout location, you can create an effective bugout bag that will meet all your needs. This will require a bunch of different types of gear and will also take a lot of consideration when it comes to how many people will need bugout bags and to what degree.

Remember, building bugout bags is a very personal process. Let's start with the bugout bag itself. For a long time, it has been assumed that a bugout bag should be huge. It should be the largest possible bag you can find and filled to the brim with survivalist goodies!

If your bugout is a straight shot down a country road for 20 miles, you might not need a bag at all! There is little chance that the road will be blocked, and you are likely to be outfitted with a vehicle that can get around that blockage.

However, if you are bugging out from NYC and you are headed 80 miles west to a secluded area, then yes, you are going to need quite the bag to make that journey; even if you are in a car, that's a long way! So, the conditions of your bugout will largely determine the type of bag you need.

Paratus 3 Day Operators Pack by 3Vgear

A large and affordable modular backpack, this model is one of my favorites to recommend because it is one of the largest bags you can get for the price. If you have a lot to pack, this backpack will take a chunk out of that.

If you have two or more members carrying these bags, you will be able to put a serious camp on your back and outfit people pretty effectively. It has just the serious capacity you may require, and you are going to pay in the hundreds for a similar bag that does what this one does.

This bag is especially effective because you can remove all of the parts and pieces that are affixed to the outside of the main bag. In other words, you can break this bag into parts and pieces. This makes things easier from organization to operations outside of base camp, and even when you need to ditch the larger bag because of a threat or the need to move quickly.

The Paratus features two side pouches with minimal organization and a rapid assault pack at the bottom of that bag. This can be removed and even features a sling that allows you to carry it over your shoulder. This small pack has a much better layout for organization. You could likely get away with this little pack as an EDC bag.

Rapid Assault Pack by Condor

The Rapid Assault Pack is a powerful bag that is built stronger than the Paratus. You can feel it. This bag is more durable, and the price is higher, but you get a lot out of this pack. It is set up in the same style as the Paratus with two side pouches and a small pack nestled under the main storage area. The big difference is all these sections are fixed to the bag.

There are benefits to that, and there are problems with that too! If you are looking for another big bag but not one that is framed, this might be the perfect bag for you. A framed hiking pack is another option, but that is a big undertaking and usually costs over $100.

This is a great bag and, though it costs more than the Paratus, it is still a very affordable bag for what you need in a bugout bag.

Velox II by 3Vgear

If the assault pack style is too big for you, a simpler tactical bag might do you one better! My bag is the Velox II because it answers the call to a number of different things that I need to achieve with it. It can become an effective bag for hiking, trips, get home bag, and even a high-quality bugout bag. It is a great bag.

This bag is set up differently. It is smaller and carried closer to the body. This is one of the things I like most about this bag. You have two main compartments that offer a lot of space for equipment. Then you have a smaller pouch on the top portion of the bag. I use this bag for everything, even fire starting!

Below that small portion, you have another square compartment for storing a few different kinds of things. This area I reserve for beverages, utensils, and other food and drink-related items. This way, I have quick access to fire, forks, tea, and coffee when the need arises.

You can lay your bag out however you like, but these bags are tremendous for what you need. I have put the Velox II through hell and back, and it remains a very tough bag that goes a long way when I need it to.

Incognito Bugout Bags

The downside to all of these bags is the fact that they are all very tactical looking. The look of the bag gives away a bit of its intention. For most people bugging out, that may not be an issue. However, suppose you are in a city or a highly populated and contentious area. In that case, you will not want to give way all of your intentions by having a camo assault pack on with your militarized patches showing clues to your political affiliation and other dangerous information.

Vertx makes some great bags that blend in seamlessly with other bags in a crowd. Their Commuter and Ready-Pack lines are great examples of bags that can stand as a bugout bag but also blend in without anyone ever noticing.

How you manage your bugout bag, and the type of bag you choose is a very big deal. Consider what you need to carry and the type of environments you are going to carry that bag through.

Caches Along the Way

You cannot carry everything, so it is important to use survival caches along your bugout route. These are simply hidden, waterproof containers that can be filled with all sorts of useful resources for the person bugging out. These caches are especially important to the person who is bugging out on foot. They will lighten the load exponentially.

The building of caches is pretty simple once you have the right containers and the resources to go inside of them. Beyond that, you are going to need locations that make sense. Concealment is the key because if they are found, they will be taken.

Let's Look at the Types of Items That Can be Contained in Caches:

- Food
- Water Resources
- Clothing
- Ammo
- First Aid Supplies
- Firearms
- Shoes
- Seeds
- Silver

Hiding caches in the ground is the most common. You will need a shovel and an area where you can turn over the earth and be inconspicuous. You can also hide caches in trees. If they are tall trees or well-hidden trees, your cache can be spray painted to match the bark and hidden.

If you need help finding great hiding spots for your caches, download the geocaching app we talked about in the previous section. After hunting for geocaches for a couple of weeks, you will be much better at locating good hiding spots for your survival caches.

I have seen caches that are stored in the water, too! These can be chained to large roots in an undercut bank or even chained to a deeply sunken post that you also 'install.' Caching can be as creative as you want it to be. It can be as covert as you want it to be. I have even seen things like false rocks used to cache survival items. It gets deep once you get into it.

Rally Points

The best-laid plans, well, you know how they go. Just because you create a perfect bugout plan does not mean that the outside world will go along with it. Rally points are designed to give you an option when the plan falls apart around you.

Mike Tyson was famously quoted saying, "Everyone has a plan until they get punched in the face."

Do you have a plan for when you get punched in the face? If not, then you are going to need to have rally points. Rally points are predetermined locations where your family will meet up when some kind of disruption breaks you up. This could be a group of people, an animal attack, a weather event, or something else.

Rally points can be predetermined, or they can be picked out along your way. You are looking for things that stand out in the distance. Things like cell towers, buildings, rock outcroppings, or other features that are easy to identify from afar and easy to reach.

As you progress on your bugout journey, rally points will change. Keep identifying new rally points as you go so that at a moment's notice, your family can be dispersed and then reconfigured near one of these rally points. There is tremendous potential in that. Getting everyone back together is the only way you can get back to bugging out.

Arriving

After the long journey, you find yourself face to face with a bugout location. You have made it from point A to point B in chaos, despite the odds. Whether you made it there by foot or by car, it does not matter. At that point, all that matters is that you have arrived. Now, it might seem like the perfect time to rush to the front door and dive into your bugout location.

But you have to be very careful about this. There is a bit of a process to follow when you are arriving at your bugout location.

Remember, you might not be the only person who has considered your bugout location as a place to weather the SHTF storm. Someone else may have arrived since the last time you stored important things or visited there, or even since you picked the location based on its advantageous position. If you are careful, you can find out if someone is at your location or not from a distance. That will be the safest way to find out.

There are several things that you want to avoid when approaching your bugout location.

- Walking into an occupied area
- Being seen before you see them
- Being ambushed at your location

Never forget the value of your BOL. If you have invested in this location, someone else could happen by and notice the "value" of the location. Since you are not always at your bugout location, there are times when it can be scoped out by others without you even knowing it.

One great way to know who is checking in on your bugout location is to have motion-activated trail cameras installed on your property. This will catch snapshots of what is moving around your property. Hopefully, you will see plenty of deer and turkey. You do not want to see a bunch of kids or a single person lurking around looking in windows. Of course, this would be great intelligence if you knew this ahead of time.

Let's Look at the Simple but Cautious Approach you Should Take When Arriving at Your Bugout Location:

- Find a vantage point that gives you the best view of your bugout location. This is a place you can find now, so you know exactly where you are going when the time comes. This location should be far enough that you need an optic to see it well.
- Setup a small but straight forward camp which can be quickly set up and broken down.
- Watch this location for at least 4 hours or until

sundown. Traveling to the location in the cover of night is a huge benefit.

- Clear every room in the home before settling in for the night.
- Practice serious light discipline, i.e., do not use any flashlights that first night.
- Sleep in shifts the first night to ensure that someone is always up your first night in the bugout. Depending on how you feel about the safety of your BOL, you might want to do this as a nightly precaution.

If you make it this far, then you are going to be sitting in your bugout location. Hopefully, you have chosen an effective location that offers you all that we have talked about. As far as I am concerned, this is a success when it comes to bugout planning and execution.

Why Not Just Live at the Bugout Location?

There is one bugout question that I am asked all the time. This question is kind of frustrating, but it comes from a place of misunderstanding. It usually goes something like this:

"Why can't I just live at my bugout location?"

Neither situation is possible. You cannot just live at your bugout location because then it is not your bugout location.

The bugout plan is based on the idea that where you are living right now could become hazardous or untenable. It does not matter if you live in the suburbs of a highly populated city or if you live off a gravel road in the country. Numerous situations could cause either location to become untenable.

Things like earthquakes, floods, radiological disasters, and even simple house fires can turn your "BUGOUT" location in paradise into a wasteland. Where do you go in an emergency if you already live at your bugout location? Where do you bug out to when your bugout location is under attack. Therefore, you simply cannot live at your bugout location. It is impossible because a bugout location is not a permanent residence. It is a plan to seek another living space if your primary residence is threatened or too much of a risk.

While it might sound like a great idea to simply sell your suburban home and move to a bugout location, it is not possible. The BOL is not a permanent situation. Believing you live at your bugout location might be more dangerous than living in the city itself! At least in the city, you could have a bugout cabin in the woods. If your home is the bugout cabin in the woods and you do not have another option when the cabin is knocked down, you are just left with the woods and the cold and whatever else lurks. Do not take this shortcut and make this mistake.

KEY CHAPTER CONCEPTS:

- Do not build a bugout bag until you know where you are going.
- Create a few bugout routes.
- Choose the right bag for the job.
- Plan and hide some survival caches if you have a long and arduous bug out ahead of you.
- Understand and identify rally points along your bugout route to keep you and yours together.
- Have a process for inspecting your BOL upon arrival.

NOW FOR THE BEST PART!

You get to help our community by giving this book a review.

Many preppers, just like you, know how hard it is to find current, concise, and useful information, especially when starting. Not only will your review help them on their prepping journey, but the information you direct them to might also save their lives!

Do another prepper a favor and leave a review talking about the information you found, what you liked about the book, and how it helped you... even if it is just a sentence or two!

Customer Reviews

⭐⭐⭐⭐⭐ 2
5.0 out of 5 stars ▾

5 star	100%
4 star	0%
3 star	0%
2 star	0%
1 star	0%

Share your thoughts with other customers

Write a customer review ⬅

See all verified purchase reviews ›

I am so very appreciative of your review, as it truly makes a difference in our community.

Thank you from the bottom of my heart for purchasing this book. I hope our paths cross again in the future.

Scan this QR code and leave a brief review on Amazon.

CONCLUSION

For years I have been teaching people how to prepare for tough times. With all honesty, I can say that I have never seen a nation more prepared for chaos. While the laundry list of issues reads like a dictionary, it is safe to say that we have every opportunity to see chaos in the suburbs.

We are living through a moment in American history when the very pillars of what holds our Nation up are cracked at the foundation. Now, I am not a fear monger. I could have motivated you with fear throughout this book, but I have always preferred enlightening and informing people and allowing them to see the writing on the wall.

You see the writing, don't you? That is probably what brought you here. Look at all of these chapters as buckets. By this point, you should have a clear understanding of each of these buckets and how you can fill them. Over the next few months, you should focus on filling each of these buckets little by little.

Now that you know how to stock your pantry and store water, you have the skills to sustain your family for months at a time, if not years! Think about the power in that. You also know how to gain the skills to look after your family regarding medical care and first aid. Stopping bleeding and caring for the sick is a game-changer.

This book has pushed you towards a life of self-reliance and independence, and now it is time for you to take action. Now that you have the blueprint, you can start filling buckets and preparing for SHTF in the suburbs.

In many ways, I admire you. You are about to start down one of the most rewarding paths in life. It is the path of fortification and preparedness. You might think you are just fortifying your pantry and your home, but the reality is, you are revealing a better lifestyle for you and yours.

Thank you so much for taking the time to read When Crisis Hits Suburbia. Please leave a positive review if you enjoyed this book. I hope you find the time and the will to act on your preparedness goals.

T. Riley

A SPECIAL GIFT TO MY READERS
EMERGENCY INFORMATION PLANNER

If you haven't already, don't forget to access your free
Emergency Information Planner

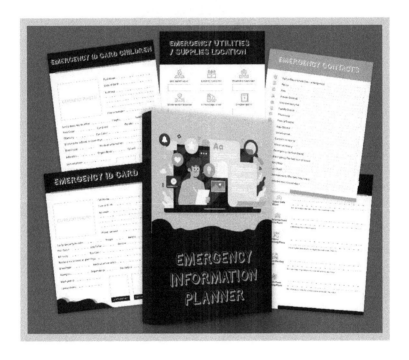

Follow the link below to receive your copy:

www.tedrileyauthor.com

Or by accessing the QR code:

Scan me

You can also join our Facebook community Suburban Prepping with Ted, or contact me directly via ted@tedrileyauthor.com.

REFERENCES

Ballard, K., 2020. *The Ultimate Prepper First Aid Kit (Full Supplies List)*. [online] The Preparedness Experience. Available at: <https://thepreparednessexperience.com/prepper-first-aid-kit/> [Accessed 22 July 2020].

Brindle, D., 2020. *53 Essential Bug Out Bag Supplies: How To Build A Suburban "Go Bag" You Can Rely Upon*. 2nd ed. p.126.

Bug Out Bag Builder. 2020. *Important Documents To Keep Checklist*. [online] Available at: <https://www.bugoutbagbuilder.com/learning-tutorials/important-documents#:~:text=If%20an%20emergency%20-forces%20you,are%20part%20of%20your%20grab> [Accessed 14 June 2020].

2000. *Centers For Disease Control And Prevention*. Atlanta, GA: Centers for Disease Control and Prevention.

2004. *Dietary Reference Intakes For Energy, Carbohydrate, Fiber, Fat, Fatty Acids, Cholesterol, Protein, And Amino Acids (Macronutrients)*. Washington: National Academies Press.

2020. [online] Available at: <https://www.fema.gov/emergency-managers/national-preparedness/plan> [Accessed 17 June 2020].

Garden, H., HowStuffWorks, Garden, Improvement, DIY and Safety, 2020. *Home-Security Tips*. [online] HowStuffWorks. Available at: <https://home.howstuffworks.com/home-improvement/household-safety/home-security-tips.htm> [Accessed 3 August 2020].

Illanes, F., 2020. *9 Critical Essentials For Choosing The Perfect Bug Out Location*. [online] Ready To Go Survival. Available at: <https://readytogosurvival.com/bug-out-location/> [Accessed 8 June 2020].

Redcross.org. 2020. [online] Available at: <https://www.redcross.org/content/dam/redcross/atg/PDF_s/Preparedness___Disaster_Recovery/Disaster_Preparedness/Food_Safety/Food_and_Water-English.revised_7-09.pdf> [Accessed 21 June 2020].

The Prepared. 2020. *Survival First Aid Kit Checklist*. [online] Available at: <https://theprepared.com/bug-out-bags/guides/first-aid-kit-list/> [Accessed 26 July 2020].

The Provident Prepper. 2020. *The Provident Prepper Action Plans | The Provident Prepper*. [online] Available at: <https://

theprovidentprepper.org/the-provident-prepper/>
[Accessed 29 August 2020].

Uspreppers.com. 2020. *Off-Grid Power For Preppers.* [online] Available at: <https://uspreppers.com/off-grid-power-for-preppers/> [Accessed 12 August 2020].

Walton, J., 2020. *Five Prepper Must-Haves For SHTF Hygiene - Apartment Prepper.* [online] Apartment Prepper. Available at: <https://apartmentprepper.com/five-prepper-must-haves-shtf-hygiene/> [Accessed 18 August 2020].

Milton Keynes UK
Ingram Content Group UK Ltd.
UKHW040037160324
439374UK00005B/329